FREE TO A GOOD HOME

Dagger Editions is an imprint of Caitlin Press
8100 Alderwood Road,
Halfmoon Bay, BC V0N 1Y1
www.daggereditions.com

Text and cover design by Gerilee McBride Design
Edited by Susan Safyan

Printed in Canada

Caitlin Press Inc. acknowledges financial support from the
Government of Canada and the Canada Council for the Arts, and the
Province of British Columbia through the British Columbia Arts
Council and the Book Publisher's Tax Credit.

Library and Archives Canada Cataloguing in Publication:

Torti, Jules, 1974–, author
Free to a good home : with room for improvement / Jules Torti.

ISBN 978-1-987915-60-0 (softcover)

1. Torti, Jules, 1974–. 2. Torti, Jules, 1974– —Travel. 3. Self-realization.
4. Self-actualization (Psychology). 5. Women—Canada—Biography. I. Title.

CT310.T63A3 2019   305.4092   C2018-905973-7

Free
to a
Good Home

with room
for improvement

JULES TORTI

DAGGER EDITIONS

Praise for *Free to a Good Home*

"Jules Torti takes you on a wild spin of a joy ride through her life
as she looks for a place to call home."

—Laurie Gough, author of *Kiss the Sunset Pig,*
Kite Strings of the Southern Cross and *Stolen Child*

"A walker, a talker and one helluva writer. An avid explorer of
this flawed and fabulous world, a fearless and hilarious examiner of the
heart's mysteries, Jules Torti is a brilliant dynamo who reminds
us that the optimism of youth and the courage to be true to oneself are
shining examples of how to live large, go big *and* find a forever home
and true love. Unless you are a terminally timid wannabe writer
with envy issues or a judgey prune with a pickle up your bum,
you'll love this wonderful book!"

—Caroline Woodward, author of *Singing Away the Dark* and
Light Years: Memoir of a Modern Lighthouse Keeper

"As a touring musician, I thought I had a flurry of road stories to tell,
but Jules must have lived five lives before she was twenty-nine to
have experienced all this so far. Her story is one that will resonate
with anyone with the taste for travel but a longing for home.
Wherever and whomever that may be."

—Lisa MacIsaac, Madison Violet

"A must read for anyone wanting to say *Yes!* to life.
In *Free to a Good Home*, Jules Torti tells the tall story of her life,
her work with chimps at the Jane Goodall Institute and in the Congo,
and her pursuit for a perfect home and partner. Her chapters on Africa
will resonate with anyone in love with the continent or travel.
Torti brilliantly captures the sights, sounds and tastes of Uganda
and readers will be moved by the personalities, and sometimes
heartbreaking pasts, of these unforgettable chimps."

—Teresa O'Kane, author of *Safari Jema: A Journey of Love and
Adventure from Casablanca to Cape Town*

Free to a good ~~home~~. Shack. Casa. Roost. Pad. Quarters. Crib.
Sanctuary. Headquarters. Villa. Base camp. Fountainhead.
Habitat. Condo. Flat. Co-op. Den. Digs. Flop. Hearth. Dwelling.
Domicile. Crash pad. Lodging. Haz. Atelier. Shtëpi. Huis. Maja.
Talo. Maison. Haus. Dom. Ruma. Whare. Indlu. 房屋. Dům
obytný. Kuća. بَيْت.

For Kim, because she is everything. She is my home.

Contents...Under Pressure

Foreword
by Jann Arden

JULES TORTI HAS A MUCH BETTER memory than I do. She can recall our very first shreds of correspondence like it was yesterday. It's all pretty vague to me, the dates and the places, the starts and stops of all the wonderful words that have flown between us these past…well, it's seeping well into the second decade as I write this.

What I do remember, vividly, is Jules herself. The impact her meanderings had on my heart and mind. She never ceased to amaze, entertain and dazzle me with her tall but very true tales about where in the heck she was and what in the heck she was seeing, feeling, eating, drinking and dreaming. I was always transported through time and space, finding myself sitting right beside her as I pored over her letters. I was dumbfounded by the incredible vulnerability she showed and how completely transparent she was with her heart and soul.

I loved her writing. I did from the very beginning. And I love this book.

Free to a Good Home, for me, is the absolute best part of Jules Torti. This book is so damn funny and so damn real. Her descriptions of the people she knows well, or even the ones who are but brief encounters, always reel you in. The places she has travelled to come to life in a way that I've never quite experienced before in the written word. Quirky comes to mind—original, one of a kind. Jules is—well, Jules. She somehow manages to describe things in an unexpected fashion and in a language that is truly original and welcoming.

I want to jump into this book every few pages and wander around with a flashlight just to get a better look. I WANT to be THERE.

Her recurring theme of home resonates with me at every turn. I have travelled all my life with my work, and my idea of home has changed throughout the years—as many times as my hairstyles. Jules's search for the meaning of home and the value of home and the essence of home stretches my heart out into places I've not yet been. We spend our lives looking for whatever that is, and I think eventually we all realize that it's not a place at all, but a state of mind.

Free to a Good Home is one of those books you want to eat. You want to crawl inside of it and live there and not come out for weeks on end. I know you'll enjoy it as much as I did, and if you don't, well, I don't think we could ever be friends.

Home is…well, you'll figure out just like Jules did, and you'll keep figuring it out for the rest of your life.

1.

Spirograph

If I started my story in the Congo, you might not follow. If I began in Uganda, you might not get it either. If I opened with my time spent in the soggy Costa Rican jungle, you'd probably have a better understanding. But if I scrolled back to age six, then you'd see.

Although my path isn't linear (in fact, it resembles a Spirograph doodle), it started long ago. It began quite simply on an unpaved countryside road in southwestern Ontario, among the corn and tobacco-fringed fields of the appropriately named village of Mount Pleasant. Our GPS coordinates were: three cornfields behind the Sunset Drive-In theatre. The Sunset's grainy screen was visible from our front step, and somehow my walkie-talkie set could pick up the audio.

I've spent a lot of time wishing I were "there," instead of the spot I was in. I've sent hundreds of postcards from the middle of nowhere that gushed, "Wish you were here!" For most of 2017, I wasn't there *or* here—I was suspended like a spider on a swinging thread that hadn't yet found its attachment site.

But now I'm here, and that Spirograph has come full circle.

This is what I mean:

I originally thought "my book" was going to be about a darling 155-year-old stone cottage on the riverbank in the old textile town of Galt, Ontario.

But it was after being in Africa that I was certain this imaginary book of mine would be about the chimpanzees I had encountered. How could I not go all Beryl Markham or Karen Blixen and write my own take on *Out of Africa*?

My early-dawn production of making breakfast for two dozen chimps in the Congo inspired foodie-evangelism book fantasies. I'd already named this book *What's Eating Me?* but I rethought this after remembering my bout with intestinal parasites (round-worms, tapeworms and some other angry protozoa) after three months in the jungle. When I casually mentioned a potential food memoir to a friend, she was nonplussed. I bragged about my "experience" writing nearly a hundred thoughtful TripAdvisor restaurant reviews. "You're not a chef. Why would anyone care what you think about a hamburger?" Come to think of it, that person wasn't a friend at all. She was an ex-girlfriend, and for good reason.

My epiphanies continued, and the book ideas kept coming, like pesky mosquitoes into a tent at dawn. I had just retired from seventeen years as a massage therapist and thought I could write *Touch and Go* or *How I Was Rubbed the Wrong Way in the Massage Industry*. But there's this sticky confidentiality thing between massage therapy clients and health-care providers, so a lot of the book would have to be blacked out. And to be honest, I was semi-bored at the thought of revisiting those dimly lit, Enya-and-peppermint-oil-infused decades.

All these things fit in my puzzle though. Sometimes you can't find a piece for a while and then it's under the couch because the cat played hockey with it one night. Other times you find a piece that almost fits, so you jam it in. It's similar enough to the other pieces to go unnoticed to the untrained eye. Maybe these are the truly interesting pieces, and you need hindsight to see the whole picture. If I were to write one specific book without all these puzzle pieces, it would be like going to the Caribbean and not mentioning the sea, the sand, the rum or pineapples. Or how fabulous Johnny Depp is as a pirate.

And then, while running one day, I saw a For Sale sign, and I knew immediately that I was meant to write about finding one particular house. The one I am happily sitting in right now. My book was going to be about my ongoing search to find my next forwarding address. I have always had my very own homing instinct for a person and a place, an invisible draw to somebody and someplace.

I have been, for most of my life, free to a good home.

2

RR#2

MINE WAS A NORMAL enough childhood, as far as we were concerned—"we" being me, my younger, then-bratty sister, Kiley (spelling unofficially changed to Kylie during the Kylie Minogue "Locomotion" years), and my even younger tagalong brother, Dax. I've only met one other Dax, and there was a Dax character on *Deep Space Nine* or one of those *Star Trek* spinoffs.

I say we thought we were normal because in the country, there's not a lot of opportunity for comparison. We thought everybody lived on roads like ours—where you were related to everyone on them. And in Mount Pleasant, this was true. Our great-grandmother lived right beside us. Nan Chapin (my mom's mom) lived farther up the road. Aunts and uncles at the top of the road swapped houses a few times back and forth, one of those houses being the one my mom was born in. There were second cousins on the other side of the tracks.

My sense of "normal" was first challenged when talk of bath time was brought up in a conversation years later. I had casually mentioned that we shared baths in the country. We had a well, and you'd think we were living in present-day California, with the rations my parents imposed upon us. To save water, all five of us would take turns in the bathtub over the course of an hour and a half. The lucky one who remembered to call dibs on first bath early in the day had the most pristine experience. Suds (created by a generous squirt of green Palmolive dish soap) would be spilling over the sides, humidity fogging the mirror. Last bath would be a lukewarm affair, bubbles long dissolved, and if the three women in the house were of shaving age, there could be an accidental spill of the glass dish used to dip the razor and rinse the stubble. Apologies to the next unsuspecting bather. My dad was usually the sacrificial lamb (meaning last bath), but the rest of us battled it out. Sometimes, even if numbers were fairly called out, somebody would take too long and there would have to be an intervention.

Though I dreamed of having a Slip 'N Slide (basically an over-priced yellow sheet of plastic used as a wet runway to slide end to end on), advertised on commercials as endless fun in the sun—no way. "What a waste of water!" We had greater thrills anyway—my grandfather irrigated the tobacco field across the road from us with the world's biggest sprinkler known to childkind. This thing would send out a thirty-foot arc of firehose spray. When the wall of water hit you, the force could actually knock you down. The water came from a nearby pond, so while it was refreshing, you inadvertently ended up with bits of duckweed and other pond debris in your swimsuit. Running through the irrigation spray between tobacco plants and rows involved deft footwork, as we were also half-blind from the water and whipped by the broad tobacco leaves.

So maybe this part wasn't normal. But we were homesteaders before it was a thing. We were off-grid before it became a hipster movement. All this media attention about conserving water and showering in non-peak hours—we'd been doing that since the seventies. It wasn't weird to us because Nan Torti—my dad's mother, who lived in the city—didn't even have a tub. She had a double-basin kitchen sink in an old wartime house in Eagle Place where she had "bird baths." And Nan Torti was a scrumper before I even knew such a term existed. Scrumping is the act of foraging for windfall fruit or helping yourself to leftover, left-behind veg in a farmer's field. It's stealing with pseudo-permission.

Nan Chapin (again, that's my mom's mom, in case the family tree branches are getting tangled in your hair) had built a house in the mid-1980s and went for a luxury spa bath. It was her treat for enduring a 24-7 pig-manure existence on their farm. My grand-father showered downstairs in a stall by the chest freezer (full of Deep'n Delicious cakes) while Nan had a "Calgon, take me away" experience upstairs in the palatial master bath with whirlpool tub and bidet. We never really knew what the bidet was for, but if you cranked it just so, you could make the water hit the ceiling, and that was great fun. And if my grandfather was on a hunting or fishing trip with the guys, we took turns sleeping over with Nan. We never had to share bathwater at Nan's, even though she had a well too.

My great-grandmother had a proper bath and shower, but we never, ever used it. What I can tell you is this: for all the years that she was alive, she was dedicated to the Zest brand. There was always, always, always a bar of Zest soap on the bathroom sink. To this day, a whiff of Zest and I can hear her cackling away on the party line (which, for those under forty, was like a conference call before conference calls were invented).

So what was normal? A bird bath or a bath with someone else's picky shaving stubble and Palmolive residue? In elementary school you didn't tend to talk about baths at recess.

Everything else was normal. I'd enrich my word power thanks to *Reader's Digest*. Kiley and I would freak ourselves out (usually on a weekly basis) looking at my mom's big red health encyclopedia with its glossy colour images of eye surgery and live birth. The eye surgery pictures were great to pull out from under the table to quickly gross out Dax so we could inhale the last of the McCain fries while he ran out of the room to fake barf.

We had lousy television reception. On a very good night, our family had maybe five channels available to us. If there was any hint of wind or flurries or a crow flying overhead, we had a snowy screen. Not that there was much to watch in those days. It was either *The Jetsons* or *The Flintstones*, *Little House on the Prairie* or *Magnum, P.I.*

Otherwise, we wanted for very few things. We had it all, really: a pollywog-filled pond behind the house, and train tracks that we walked upon like balance beams. We tried flattening pennies on those same tracks, but the train was so infrequent we usually forgot about the pennies until "next time." I suppose we had a little bit of city-kid envy.

Making money in the country involved hard labour, unlike the urban alternatives—lemonade stand, paper route. Dax and I earned a steady income taking an S.O.S pad to the whitewalls of my dad's baby-blue Cutlass Supreme. We'd Turtle Wax the tires too—then shine up our BMXs with the same attention but without pay. For piecework, we would pick gravel out of the grass after the snow melted (whenever my grandfather plowed the drive, he routinely plowed the gravel too, onto the grass). Seasonally, we could also pick up pine cones in the woods, where my dad cut the grass with a push mower. If you've ever cut grass in a pine cone–filled forest, you'll know that it's like being hit by hot shrapnel when those cones fire out the side or back of the mower.

My earliest form of entrepreneurial income in elementary school, however, was illustrating birthday cards with Garfield on them. That is, until a cranky art teacher told me I could be sued for copyright violations, even though I was eight and had no idea what copyright even meant, and I was selling my cards to relatives. At Christmas, I taped tiny squares of text and coloured drawings of Garfield or our Persian cat to a long green Woolco ribbon. This way, the buyer could hang the story prominently in their home. Who wouldn't want to do this? I learned the art of fancy ribboning too. My mom showed me how to splay the scissors and run them along the ribbon length to give it a tight curl.

Our cat, Moker (pronounced like "smoker" without the "s"), was extremely outdoorsy. According to my drawings, she was always busy snowmobiling and cross-country skiing. When she wasn't skiing, we would give her haircuts, trimming her wily whiskers to nubs. We used her clipped whiskers as the ultimate tickling weapons against each other. Before you call PETA, we didn't know better. We cut each other's bangs too, so we all looked the part.

We had a devoted dog, Xanadu, who was a Benji knock-off. He was free to a good home too. Really *free*, as he was a roadside drop-off. For some peculiar reason, people still to this day think it's a reasonable thing to drop off a cat or dog in the country because it will magically find shelter. I get doing this with ex-girlfriends, but a little pup? Shame.

I had a microscope for looking at scabs (and probably boogers), just like Margaret Atwood's Elaine Risley, the protagonist in *Cat's Eye*. Dax had a telescope and a fish tank. Jointly we had shelves of books, lizards (who came to us already named Bob and Doug), loonie-sized turtles, comics, stickers, NHL cards and a Snoopy slushy machine (the most coveted item from the Consumers Distributing holiday catalogue). Kiley had a whole herd of

My Little Ponies and sea monkeys (though we could never teach them to play baseball like the packaging promised). We each had cassette players, bikes, skis, skates, soccer balls—my dad even had a T-ball stand made for us. Dax has a scar across his head to prove it. I had a three-quarter-sleeve Michael Jackson concert T-shirt. Hot damn, what else did I need?

Kiley thought we were poor, though. The Valade family on Pleasant Ridge Road had *everything*. "They are the richest people in the world!" declared Kiley. The Valades had a TV in their kitchen (it had a ten-inch screen that required a telescope to see from the far end of the kitchen), a pinball machine in their basement and a swimming pool. And their mother made them homemade ice cream sandwiches. We, on the other hand, were so hard done by. We had to subject ourselves to the public pools with the floating Band-Aids. Sometimes Kiley would run away because we were "poor." Never far, though. We could always see her, bag packed, sitting on the train tracks in a huff—always entirely visible from our kitchen window. Dax and I would wave crazily at her and rat her out to my mom that she had run away again. We made quick and lofty plans for her bedroom (Dax and

....

We were only ten kilometres from Calbeck's grocery store, but ten kilometres in the stuffy Cutlass Supreme or my mom's wood-panelled Pinto seemed like a cross-Canada journey. There was no pizza delivery service in our neighbourhood. Instead, we had to call in our order, get in the Cutlass or the Pinto, drive to Gigi's Pizza—the closest pizzeria, near Calbeck's—and wait in the steamy-windowed, yeast-filled humidity of Gigi's storefront. We'd wrap the large pizza in blankets to retain the heat and sneakily help ourselves to bits of crust or cheese—whatever we could pull out of the quarter-sized ventilation hole in the side of the pizza box—in between making cat and dog paw prints with the heels of our hands on the fogged windows in the back seat.

More often, we'd have frozen McCain personal-sized pan pizzas. Personally, I didn't think the size was ever big enough, and the cheese-to-sauce-to-crust ratio was dismal. But this was off-grid, no-pizza-delivery living. •

I shared one with bunks at that point), but Kiley always returned, usually just before dinner. (She is air-strangling me as she reads this, probably.)

I didn't run away, but I still harboured fantasies about "somewhere else." At a certain age, my radius extended only as far as Jerseyville (thirty minutes away), where we went to a Chinese restaurant on the highway for chow mein noodles dipped in plum sauce and deep-fried pineapple-chicken balls in that heavenly thick neon-yellow sauce. Lime Ridge Mall in Hamilton was pretty much a day trip (reality check: one hour away). And Canada's Wonderland amusement park in Vaughan? It was past the CN Tower—now *that* was far away.

So I didn't really know where "somewhere else" could be. In Mount Pleasant, everything was familiar. Lloyd delivered the *Brantford Expositor*. Mr. McIntyre drove the school bus and was the kind of bus driver you loved and wanted to give boxes of chocolates to at Christmas. We were the first ones on the bus and the last ones off for all our school years, so we knew all of the drivers like family. At Halloween, everyone recognized us (especially the aforementioned relatives) and made limited-production caramel apples, Smarties-studded cookies as big as Frisbees, and Nuts and Bolts, specifically for us. On a "good" Halloween, rural homeowners could count on three trick-or-treaters: us. And maybe an interloper from a nearby side road, freeloading on our territory.

On Pleasant Ridge Road, the most lucrative stretch for trick-or-treaters, residents knew us as Sandra Chapin's kids ("Oh gosh, you have her smile!") or Larry Torti's kids ("Your dad, he played hockey with the Foresters, right? You have his smile!"). Everyone knew each other, just like on *Cheers* but in a farm-setting kind of way. My parents built our brick ranch house, and my great-grandmother still lived in the house she was born in. We didn't know anything different. Our road was eventually named the Arthur Side Road after my great-grandparents. It takes a lot of staying power to earn that.

There were rarely "new kids" at Mount Pleasant Public School, but when there were—wow! *Where* did you come from? Why did people move? I didn't know anyone who had. Everyone on our road just stayed. In grade three, my classmate Jeremy Guest left Mount Pleasant. It seemed abrupt but probably wasn't. His family was moving to Egypt, wherever that was. I figured it had to be somewhere just past the Chinese restaurant or maybe beyond Canada's Wonderland. My mom said his dad worked for Ontario Hydro and had to move because of his job. At night, Kiley and I carried on hushed conversations: "What if Dad gets a job in Egypt?" (He didn't.) When Jeremy returned almost ten years later, I couldn't believe it. Who moves and comes back? He showed me a picture of him sandboarding in the desert dunes. (I still have that picture.) He talked about playing with a Ouija board in the pyramids in the still-mystical, to me, Egypt. The pyramids!

I once had my own Ouija experience too—not at the pyramids, but at Nan Chapin's kitchen table.

My guest column in Shelia Smith's weekly Countryside feature in the *Brantford Expositor* was my most notable achievement by age nine. Shelia was the most famous naturalist I knew next to Lorne Greene. I read her column about birds and Botswana every weekend, and wished I could bird alongside her. And I eventually did—after I wrote her an old-fashioned letter, she invited me to join her on a Christmas bird count in nearby Simcoe; it was a defining first star-struck moment. She was my personal celebrity and I ate up every bit of her company and knowledge. We tromped in the woods with a Thermos of hot tea and "Figgy Newtons" (as she referred to them), documenting purple finches and nuthatches by the dozen.

I was the youngest member of the Brantford Nature Club then; everyone else had decades on me. We sang "O Canada" at the beginning of each meeting, ate store-bought cookies and drank Styrofoam-cupped tea during slide shows presented by group members or local naturalists like Shelia.

She came to my school and demonstrated bird banding, and we built birdhouses for bluebirds. I was on cloud nine. When she gave me a copy of Roger Tory Peterson's bird guide (the one I still use today), I was certain I would become just like her. Or Roger. I would be an ornithologist and tramp around the bush looking for birds all day, and then I would write about it all and doodle my day while eating Figgy Newtons with cups of tea. When Shelia asked me if I wanted to write a guest column, I knew I had made it. I mean, this was the dream! I wrote about birding with the great Shelia and nervously drew a dusky sparrow (an extinct species last seen in 1975). I toured the *Brantford Expositor* headquarters behind the scenes and was given the actual layout page of my article. (It was laminated for posterity and is rolled under our bed in a Rubbermaid container of my early journalism archives.) •

Cup of tea. Stack of Chips Ahoy! cookies and greasy fingers locked on to the moving witchcrafty piece. We'd repeatedly ask, "What is Nan's bra size?" Why I/we cared about that will never be known.

To this day, I can name all the new students who came to Mount Pleasant Elementary. They were like rock stars. And in true rock star groupie fashion, I dated them all—all two of them. I had a long-term and monogamous relationship with Robert LeBovic in grade seven and moved on to Rodney Burden in grade eight. Robert sent me sweaty notes asking if I'd like to jump in the sack, and I really had no idea why I'd want to do that. The stolen kisses were just fine. The term "lesbian" was completely off my radar then, even though I'd recently been reprimanded for asking our teacher, Mr. McFadzean, what "buggery" meant (on behalf of my classmate Tyra Foster, who was reading a Stephen King novel that used the word a few times). I'd never seen a vein pop on someone's forehead so fast.

I listened to the *Dirty Dancing* soundtrack on repeat at night, and admittedly, my thoughts were not always with Robert or Rodney. They sometimes drifted to a woman, especially while mouthing the words to Patrick Swayze's "She's Like the Wind."

Remember, I was living on a road where I was related to every person on it. I went to a tiny elementary school with the same faces for eight years on repeat. There was no Google or Netflix to assist with sexual curiosity (just my dad's *Playboy* calendar, which was easily accessed in his argyle sock drawer, and oh, did I "google" that!). There were no gays on TV aside from Tom Hanks in *Bosom Buddies*, and I knew I definitely wasn't one of those. My mom loved Liberace, but to me, he was just all sequins and Halloween-like. If that was gay, I didn't know it.

My celebrity crushes were mainly focused on River Phoenix, but there was a paparazzi photographer in a *Tiger Beat* magazine that twanged a guitar string deep inside me. She wore a white button-down shirt with buttons open a long way down. Her jeans were faded (maybe acid-washed, even?). She was holding a camera lens as long as a telescope, and her dark bangs fell over her left eye, just so. I have no idea who she was, to this day. It was a hurried look while my siblings and I were loitering at the magazine racks at the grocery store. We usually had a solid hour to skim the mags (and we were shameless, often sitting on the floor, cross-legged, with these magazines) while my mom and Nan Chapin shopped at Calbeck's. But I haven't forgotten her face.

Kiley couldn't wait for boobs, while I had already hatched a plan that involved using masking tape to hide any boobs that I might develop. Who wanted boobs? Dax certainly didn't. At the beach, he was the one in a Mickey Mouse one-piece while I ran around shirtless. All signs pointed toward a very gay son and, for sure, a gay daughter.

I often fantasized about being the new *boy* at school. Once I got to be one, on the annual school-picture day. Girls were asked to stand behind the boys, who were seated on a bench. I think this was grade six—I know I had a Dallas Cowboys sweatshirt on. I queued up with the taller girls in the second row but was asked to kindly take my place on the bench with the boys. I was thrilled. (Still am to this day.) My tomboyishness had completely fooled the photographer, and for posterity, there I sit, legs spread wide, Dallas Cowboys shirt on, grinning with the boys. But what did I know?

What were my wants when I was in elementary school?

- A reliable source for Mexican jumping beans.

- An attic.

- A second-floor bedroom with one of those race-car beds.

- Left-handedness.

- One different-coloured eye (preference: one green, one blue).

- That Play-Doh hairdresser set where you could crank Play-Doh through heads and make kooky hair.

- An endless supply of Mrs. Kellam's homemade Nuts and Bolts—Mrs. Kellam nailed that perfect marriage of garlic salt, soya and butter-saturated Shreddies.

My mom had built me a dollhouse with a tiny cedar-shake roof, neatly wallpapered walls and even carpeted floors. I think it had an attic—all the good books I read had attics in them where you could find vintage things, diaries and arrowheads. I played "house" with this dollhouse—but with G.I. Joe figurines as the homeowners—and a pad of graph paper. My mom was always rearranging furniture in our house, re-wallpapering, repainting. Dax and I (with our shared quarters) would sit down and cut out blocks to represent all of our furniture—bunk beds, a dresser, a desk. We would place the blocks on the graph paper and move them about the "room" to see how we could rearrange things. Kiley did the same, and then we'd glue our final arrangement to the graph paper, indicating windows and doors (with a little semicircle on the door indicator to show which way the door opened into the room). I felt like a miniature architect. Right-handed, but still cool.

Instead of being the new kid, I'd be the kid with a new room, and that was good too.

3.
Grandmas Know Best

GROWING UP IN THE COUNTRY was all I knew.

But while sitting cross-legged in Nan Chapin's library, I naturally discovered different concepts of home, thanks to her shelves of *National Geographic* that dated back to 1920. Mostly, Dax and I searched for the boob shots of women in Malaysia or Somalia. *Nat Geo* was our cultural version of *Playboy*, I suppose, but it was definitely there, in the stale air of the library, that our world expanded. Dax and I drank warm CPlus or Tahiti Treat and spent hours deep in the pages of those magazines. Nan also had over thirty encyclopedia sets—it was like I had my own private Trinity College. I'm surprised she didn't have a copy of the Book of Kells under glass.

My worldly exposure then was entirely courtesy of *National Geographic*. And *National Enquirer*—but that was thanks to my great-grandmother's literary preferences (my Party Line Grandma). Party Line Grandma called them her "smut magazines." Our reading habits had a healthy balance of Botswana safaris and

Arctic explorations diluted by three-hundred-pound-alien-baby stories. We weren't allowed to say "smut" at home, even though Grandma told us it was also something corn got, like a fungus. And I was supposed to relay that info to my city Nan, who tried to feed us cattle corn one night. (Disclaimer for city folk: Cattle or pig corn is a far stretch from a nice hot cob of peaches and cream. It's tough and starchy and no amount of butter can better it.)

This is why we needed our team of grandmothers to keep us on the straight and narrow with their different areas of expertise. Their curriculum was as varied as it was enlightening, but each grandmother showed us a version of the world that the others couldn't.

Nan Torti gained popularity points when she got cable television. Our cartoon options grew tenfold. She had MuchMusic, Arsenio Hall and *The Ant and the Aardvark*. She had pizza delivery too—although we usually maximized our fast-food treat by choosing Fast Eddie's, a.k.a. "Fat Eddie's." You could get thirty-nine-cent fries, forty-nine-cent hamburgers and dollar shakes. It meant we could double up on everything. It was the fastest way to increase your cholesterol and possibly have a heart attack as a child for just under three dollars.

Party Line Grandma lived right next door to us, and for two years we hopped off the school bus every day and made a beeline to her house because both my parents worked late—"late" in those days was until 6:00 p.m. Grandma kept us well fed with stuff that "normal" kids would gag over: fried smelts, fish eyes, fried puff-ball mushrooms, rabbit stew (insert Kiley, crying, though she never became vegetarian) and something called "Popeye," a thick, gluey stew with dumplings. My grandfather was a pig farmer, so pork featured large in our diets, from the chops to the hocks (insert Kiley crying here again, pig hoofs sticking out from the pot, bobbing about in the lima beans). We ate high off the hog, for sure.

But on Fridays we got to choose something from her chest freezer, which we hung over, hips balanced just so, terrified of actually toppling in, not trusting either sibling to report the incident. The freezer was full of Swanson TV dinners, something else my mom refused to buy due to sodium, artificialness and so on. I always went for the turkey dinner—it was like Christmas any old time. That whipped blob of potatoes with a tidy square of butter was something else. Shrivelled peas and uniformly cubed carrots tasted even better in those foil trays. Kiley always dug deep for the fried chicken, and Dax, well, he was the littlest, so he landed whatever the more acrobatic sisters left behind. Grandma also bought the desserts that my mom didn't (as my mom could bake anything better than the store-bought). There were foil-wrapper Swiss Rolls, pudding cups, Wagon Wheels and those Del Monte fruit cups with a quarter of a lucky cherry in the mix.

We played rounds of dominoes and Kings on the Corner while Grandma smoked dozens of Player's cigarettes. My mom always begged us never to smoke (and none of us would dream of it): "It wrinkles your face right up!" Grandma was testament to this— she was so wrinkled that she looked like Mother Teresa. Her hair was a shock of white, and without her teeth in, she looked like one of those apple-face dolls that you make out of apples left to dehydrate for several days.

We stayed in a tight perimeter at Grandma's. Most of our time was logged around her kitchen table; we were like pint-sized poker players in the smoky haze. We had time to watch one episode of *Little House on the Prairie* before dinner was ready, with the volume cranked to drown out the bubbling guppy tank. I can see the room to this day (it never changed): big pheasant feathers in a vase, black porcelain panthers on shelves, a clock that ticked louder than the guppy tank, and over a hundred salt and pepper shakers in a cabinet.

She had a lot of porcelain frogs too, including the signature one by the sink with the dish scrubber in it. And cacti, even those tall, arm-sized ones with a bazillion prickers that every now and again we'd brush up against (or get "accidentally" pushed into).

We never went into Grandma's bedroom—it was simply off limits. She was widowed early on, before I was born, and never entertained the thought of remarrying. (Note: This is pure speculation on my part.) We never, *ever* went downstairs either. It was bat-cave and batshit dark on the other side of the chest freezer.

Grandma's table always had a doily on it. (She made them on a daily basis, or she made crude slippers out of yarn. They were like wearing banana peels on your feet. Try going down wooden stairs with a pair of those suckers on. It was a surprisingly fast slip and tumble to the very bottom after just one step.) She was as arthritic as she was wrinkly—her knuckles a physical resumé of years of hard labour, picking tobacco, tending to her enormous vegetable gardens and rose bushes and scything long grass like a madwoman. She loved those gardens and routinely threatened to skin us alive for running through her rows. (My apologies to Kiley, for leaving her behind to be skinned.)

As present as her pack of cigarettes and *National Enquirer*, Grandma's table always had a bowl of Scotch mints, along with another softer white square mint with a wintergreen filling, and giant pink candies that Kiley, Dax and I each had a near-death choking experience with. We took turns swallowing those things whole. After an electric bolt of shock, our eyes bigger than they should be to stay in their sockets, we'd swallow harder and harder until the stupid candy worked its way down our straw-sized esophagi. Grandma would laugh and then cough herself into a bent-over position. We'd laugh until we farted and then resume the game we were playing.

As kids, we'd take turns "petting" her cat, Sam, with the broom. Sam was like an ottoman; she was pure white with avocado-green eyes and weighed at least twenty pounds. Instead of mewing like a normal cat to be let in, she'd simply ram her head into the aluminum screen door, popping the metal in and out like a pop can with her tank head. Sam would never sit on your lap (which was a good thing because you'd quickly lose feeling in your legs), but you could take a corn broom to her and brush her all around the room. Isn't this normal childhood stuff?

Sometimes Nan Torti and Aunt Buffer (my father's sister Cathy) came out to our house. (I should probably explain "Buffer" because it's not a common or even an ethnic name. I couldn't pronounce "Cathy" when I was a tot, and so "Cathy" came out as "Buffer." If you say the two names quickly, you'll see that they practically rhyme.) Nan Torti and Buffer were a package deal. Nan didn't drive and Buffer didn't own a car, so they'd rent a Topaz or a Taurus and make a weekend out of it and us. Nan and Buffer were so citified that everything in the country elicited a scream or panic attack or tears. They were chronically terrified of snakes, spiders, potential burglars, the darkness of night, a swaying tree branch. For two women who loved to chase storms and ambulances, they were a fearful duo. Nan always said, "If God spares me, we'll go swimming tomorrow at Earl Haig Park." "If God spares me, we'll go to Fat Eddie's." "If God spares me, I'll crochet you a Nordic knit."

When God spared us (and we weren't religious at all), we sometimes went cross-border shopping to Buffalo, when our dollar was worth a dollar and not fifty cents. Buffer and Nan bought bags and bags of stuff at Walden Galleria mall—usually matching outfits. Crushed-velvet leggings, anything with animal print and definitely anything purple. Sometimes we had to wear a few of these items under our own clothes for the border crossing. Nan, in the front passenger seat, would warn us: "Don't tell your father about this." We didn't get it—about paying duty or any wrongdoing. It was more like getting to do Halloween dress-up in the car. Kiley and I still like to tease Dax about wearing lace teddies on these border runs.

Dax didn't mind the dresses, and I thought he was so lucky to be a boy and never have to wear one. I quit Girl Guides almost exclusively because of the "dress" code. Could Dax and I somehow swap? While Nan fawned over my Brooke Shields eyebrows, she was desperate for me to get my ears pierced and my hair permed. I wanted none of it. Dax and Kiley played soap stars with Buffer's makeup (Buffer was a big fan of purple eyeshadow, so they adopted her palette as well) while I admired Buffer's pants-only attire and short hair. I have to give Buffer credit for my ultimate tomboy decision to lop all my hair off. Not surprisingly, my dad still has that blond ponytail in a china cabinet with our baby shoes dipped in bronze and a few baby molars.

This transformative hairdo was obviously way before that elementary school photo where I was moved to the bench to be seated with the boys. The haircut happened in grade three or so, and I went from a little princess who slept in a canopy bed with pink things to a rough-and-tumble tomboy with scratches and scars to prove it. I was often mistaken for my parents' son and relished every moment.

We spent *a lot* of time with Nan and Buffer. Buffer was definitely not a tomboy or remotely gay. She just had short hair and a lot of pants, and I thought that was the way to go. Nan and Buffer were a couple in our minds—it didn't seem strange to us that there wasn't a grandfather or uncle in the mix. They gave us cards that read "Love from the two of us" on the front or "From the both of us," as though they were a couple. But they weren't, even though they slept in the same bed—and didn't have to. Nan's house had three bedrooms, but Nan and Buffer slept with each other.

Ruth, Nan Torti's sister, who lived near London, Ontario, was as crass as Nan; they both swore like truckers. Nan Chapin had a different style of swearing (more "Jesus Christ" or "for Chrissakes" or "bullshit"). Nan Torti, being religious and all, didn't take the Lord's name in vain, but good God, she felt free to say everything else.

Aunt Ruth and I had a special kinship, as we both shared a birthday on September 18. She always called me on the date, and her voice was like sweet, honeyed gravel. She was widowed early on too, but I do have a few flashes of Uncle Jack in my head, ball cap tipped up, sitting on his chugging Massey Ferguson tractor. King, their German shepherd, was always on his heels. As was I. Here, on their dill farm, was the first time I saw a chicken run around with its head cut off (Kiley, crying). They always had tiny kittens in the barn, and we were permanently itchy from jumping in the haystacks.

The last time I saw Jack was a weekend when we went to the London Farmers' Market. He gave me one of those rubber balls with three stripes: blue, white, red. I was maybe five. I was thrilled to ride in the back of the pickup with King, until my baseball hat blew off on the highway and was run over by two cars that trailed us. Jack swung around, pulling a tight U-ey, and retrieved it for me, a little more flattened but still good all the same.

We went back to Ruth's for pork chops (that was her signature thing), and by then Nan and Ruth were fighting like rutting deer. Always. They'd be pleasant as pie for the first hour and then get into it. I have no idea what they had rows about, but we'd snicker and pretend to be unaware, with our *Archie* comics pressed to our faces.

Ruth could carry on a cutthroat yelling match with Nan and simultaneously make the best chocolate shakes ever. She had a pastel-green Hamilton Beach mixer—the kind with the stainless-steel mixing cup that would get all frosty and make your hands itchy from the cold—and she made us all shakes, even before dinner. Later that night (I may be amalgamating memories here) we had a bonfire, and Ruth went inside to get us something to toast marshmallows with. She found a meat fork and thought it was safest for her to do the toasting for us, as the handle was really short. She scorched the first one and offered to eat it because it wasn't perfect. Then we all watched as Aunt Ruth settled those molten-hot meat fork tines on her lips, oblivious. It's one thing to sacrifice the roof of your mouth to a lava-hot marshmallow—but this was a broiled fork! She had two fork-tine lines branded on her lips for the rest of the week. It somehow did not impede her swearing streaks.

Sleepovers took a dramatic turn after 1984. Twisters often ripped through the London area, but 1984 was a doozy, and Nan, faint of heart as she was, was worried about God sparing her on those drives into the eye of the storm. We were stationed at RR#2 with Nan and Buffer—my dad probably had a hockey tournament out of town. Tornado warnings were issued on the local radio station, CKPC, which Nan had blaring as soon as the clouds turned bruised on the horizon. She knew where the closest road culvert was located so we could take shelter, and we knew where the culvert was too, because it was awesome for spiderwebs and echoing songs or screams. Buffer was a self-proclaimed meteorologist (in addition to her admin work at the police station as a civilian), and she sat us down for a funnel cloud and Fujita scale F5 lesson.

Again, all highly normal family behaviour. Love, from the both of us, during this Fujita. Somebody help Dax take his purple eyeshadow off.

While random lessons in frying puffballs, religion, stealth cross-border shopping tactics and makeup application seemed inconsequential at the time, a fast-forward to my present self demonstrates distinct links to those precious grandmother tutorials. *National Geographic* had entered my bloodstream at a greater speed than *National Enquirer*, and I began to feel the need to see those stories in real time.

4.

Sounding Bored

I WAS DEFINITELY A CHILD survivor—of tornado watches, cattle corn poisoning and multiple golf-ball-sized candy-choking episodes.

But the greatest threat of all wasn't corn or those pink candies— it was the dreaded assault from Kiley's high-impact, cement-headed Cabbage Patch Kid, which ordinarily looked innocent and cheek-pinchingly cute. That thing could knock out a horse if the blow was directed correctly. I received so many head-to-head blows that it's a miracle I can still form sentences and microwave popcorn, and I had plenty of goose eggs as proof.

Kiley had such good things to steal, though—her diary being the most prized object. You never needed the tiny key to open the lock; an ice pick made quick work of it. I learned skills like this from *Magnum, P.I.*, no doubt. I did have a nicely kitted-out home-made spy kit to track Kiley with. It was a faux-alligator-skin suit-case with a red velvet interior. I think it was probably a travelling bar kit originally, but it doubled perfectly for my spy needs. I had a small gun that shot out plastic discs the size of a quarter, a microscope (not just for scabs) and a zip-lock bag of Johnson's Baby Powder, which was cocaine, of course. Because every spy needs a bag of cocaine. Did that idea come from *The Hardy Boys*? That didn't seem possible. Otherwise, all of our worldly learning came from *National Geographic*. Or, in our preteen years, Dr. Ruth, our go-to sex sage.

Every Sunday night, Dax and I would tune in to her radio show, the radio at a level that was barely audible. My brother and I shared a room for a few years, as we proved to be more compatible roommates than Kiley and me (insert Cabbage Patch battle here). I'm not sure what Kiley was doing while we were getting a full-on education with Dr. Ruth. She was clearly not into the enlightening questions from callers about erections, ejaculation, threesomes and bi-curious encounters. Dax and I ate it all up, hardly breathing until the show was over, taking mental notes of this foreign world ahead of us.

Our Dr. Ruth follow-up usually involved making lists of who we thought was hot and whom we might have sex with. It was a 100 percent celebrity list, so it was tame and pure bunk-bed fantasy talk. We made Top Ten lists for both obvious categories: hottest guys and hottest girls. This didn't seem strange to us at all—the fact that we were making crush lists for the opposite sex and the same sex. It wasn't something that had to be said aloud; it just was.

I remember Madonna, Sinead O'Connor and River Phoenix figuring large for both of us. Maybe I just admired River's simplicity in his fashion choices: white T, jeans and Converse high-tops. I had a similar style: three pairs of rugger pants (navy, burgundy, grey) and my KangaROOS runners. There seemed to be only one place to buy shoes in Brantford (Buster Brown's), and I don't think Buster carried Converse, or I would have had a pair, for sure. Bo Duke from *The Dukes of Hazzard* was on my list too. I think Dax always picked some cyborg *Star Trek* characters I wasn't wholly familiar with. I thoughtfully added the nameless paparazzi photographer with the cinder bangs, thousand-watt smile and army boots. Kelly McGillis in her aviators and snug *Top Gun* flight jacket was a no-brainer, easy duplicate for Dax and me. She took our breath away.

We both agreed on Mimi, the surfboard starlet from Jane Siberry's "Mimi on the Beach" video, too. We couldn't break the plastic tab off that VHS tape fast enough. Nobody was going to record over our Mimi on the Beach. Come to think of it, Jane was probably on our list too—what with her half-shorn hair, crimped bangs and lanky body striding through the sand dunes.

Maybe the reason Kiley didn't participate in our Top Ten sex lists or join our radio show audience was because we had locked her in her room. She was an avid sleepwalker in her tiny years, so my parents decided it was best to put a latch hook on the exterior of her bedroom door frame—to prevent midnight calls (she would politely ring the doorbell and waltz in, pyjama clad, and head back to bed after being who knows where). The lock served Dax and me too. We could quietly get a kitchen chair and, if her door was just ajar, quickly slam it and trap her. But this was never fun for long; she screamed a blood-curdler, which always successfully alerted my parents, and who could we pick on if she was locked in her room? So we'd let her out, never, ever being properly prepared for the *whack* of her doll's head or equally cement-like feet.

I also survived several punctures from the apparently designer but highly lethal wheat-sheaf table in our living room. It was a gold-coloured bundle of metal wheat with a metal braid around its centre and a circular glass top. Countless times a wayward sheath would nearly gouge our eyes out as we wrestled under the table. My dad walked into the sheath all the time. And a nice sharp jab in a socked foot left us all hopping and swearing at the table.

Yep, still a nice, normal childhood.

I jest, but growing up in the country did come with serious dangers. I survived tetanus—on a daily basis, if such things were tracked. I hopped the old rail fence behind our house every single day. I scaled the ladder with its rusty nails to a pine branch that was intended to be the foundation for a tree house one day but never was. Hide-and-go-seek in the pig barn was all about hiding in the rustiest things: old tractors, combines, manure spreader parts. Once, our cousin was run over by a tractor; another cousin was backed over by a riding lawn mower. One of the Kellam boys lost most of his hand in a farm implement. One of my older cousins had only half an arm (and I never knew why). Luckily, the most I lost was chunks of hair from climbing trees and getting in serious pine-sap fights with Kiley. The only stitches I suffered came after I went off my rocker at age two. Kaboom, right into the corner of the massive console TV (it was the size of a car, so no wonder I collided). I had a thing for standing *on* that rocker, and my chin can still prove it.

If I were to ask my dad about survival stories, he would certainly mention the VCR. We were the last family on earth to actually purchase one, but in the meantime, every other weekend was spent connecting a rental VCR from Jumbo Video. The fact that you could *rent* a VCR is historically amazing. It was twenty-five dollars for a weekend rental, and that fee included two VHS movies and a bag of the famous Jumbo Video popcorn. We'd spend two hours at Jumbo selecting movies that we could all agree upon, grazing on the free in-store popcorn until we had cankers from the salt.

Then my dad—let's just start calling him Flo, because that's how the family refers to him, to this day. There's no big story—

it was just a nickname. He's really a Larry, which we turned into singsong Lawrence and then Florence, and then, hello, Flo! We were a family of nicknames—Flo's sister was Buffer, Kiley was "Nims" or "Pumpkin," Dax was "Wheatman" or "Chucky," and I was the very flattering "Horse." My mom was "Wifey," pronounced "Wiffy" by Flo. Anyway, after two hours at the video store, and maybe another half-hour making the city run worthwhile by ordering individual pizza buns from Gigi, the games began. Flo would stand behind the console TV, flashlight in hand, teeth clenched. Dax, curious about all things electrical, would be crouched practically in Flo's armpit. The rest of us simply sat in front of the console TV, waiting for the magic to happen. There was an outrageous fee if you didn't rewind the rented videos (maybe two dollars), so Flo instilled an enormous fear into us: "Did you guys rewind those movies?" We knew how much labour was involved in rewinding a cassette tape.

Another childhood fear we had was that our house was going to blow up. My mom would warn us that if we touched the thermostat, the whole house could blow. We believed her. She didn't supply us with any references, but her eyes were wide and sure.

We didn't camp as a family (my mom was a big fan of hot baths, clean feet and hotels), but we did have an enormous canvas circus tent that once a year my dad would erect for us. It smelled like ten wet dogs. Another common dread was touching the sides of the tent. We thought that maybe this would cause an electric shock— or maybe the tent would blow up like the house. But because the tent was canvas, touching the sides made the condensation seep in. The thing was always soggy anyway. Our sleeping bags felt like sweat balls, and rarely did we last a full night in the tent. Flo would plug in a lamp for us and run a mile-long extension cord to the back of the house. We'd eat Cheezies until our molars had an inch of compressed orange on them, read our books by sixty-watt bulbs and then get the hell back to the house as soon as the first pine cone fell and slithered down the canvas roof.

Because we lived in the country, and going to the city seemed to be such an ordeal, Kiley, Dax and I were all looking for home-based business ideas. Kiley was running a highly successful and prestigious White Rabbit Club (the name later changed to the White Unicorn Club). She was in grade three and had created a membership-only club for her friends, whom she charged weekly dues. When a classmate was excluded from membership, rabbit shit hit the fan and the school principal stepped in. Kiley was to fold the club (she didn't have to pay back any dues) immediately, all because somebody felt ousted. Had this girl not ratted to her mom, Kiley would probably still be the White Rabbit Club president and CEO, with several chapters across North America.

I discovered that people would pay to walk on trails that we made along the pond with the weeping willows. My vision at age ten was to open my own nature centre right there. We lived close to the Apps' Mill Nature Centre, so my business model was based entirely on this concept. (Eventually I went on to work at Apps' for most of my high school years.) My ten-year-old self was going to operate birdwatching expeditions and stream studies with Mason jars. I maintained the trails with some of my dad's tools and mapped the area—right down to the top-secret spot where I buried three overdue library books. (I keep meaning to send the Mount Pleasant Public School library thirty bucks. I know one of the books was *The Legend of Bigfoot* and the other an NHL scrap-book, but I forget the third.)

Dax made coin from his Nintendo investment. On one of our cross-border shopping ventures with Nan and Buffer, Dax took his gravel and pine cone–picking savings and purchased a Nintendo and *Super Mario Bros.* Then he charged Kiley and me twenty-five cents a game to earn a return on his investment. Why didn't we play for free when he was distracted, sleeping or at a friend's? Because he locked the whole set up, hiding the vital electrical cords and all. He's still smart to this day, and I'd like to say he earned his PhD thanks to early strategies like this. So, thanks to Kiley and me. Financiers.

When he wasn't operating his own arcade, Dax tended to *his* garden. The deal was this: Dax would select and order the seeds from the Stokes catalogue, and my mom would pay. Dax would plant and sow, row by row, and my mom would pay. Dax would then harvest his produce (cukes, corn, tomatoes, peppers, beans, peas, sunflowers, raspberries, asparagus) and sell them to everyone else. Even to my mom.

Meanwhile, my business ideas were flopping. I toyed with the idea of a museum (in my bedroom, of course) and started labelling all my arrowheads, pickled baby opossums (preserved in formaldehyde that came from Dwayne the pharmacist at Telfer Place, the retirement home where my mom worked as a secretary), skunk cabbage and bird skulls. I recorded episodes of *Lorne Greene's New Wilderness* with my cassette recorder, which I could play for visitors to the museum. It was tricky to stop and start with all the commercials, ensuring that I hit Play and Record simultaneously and not just Play.

I also recorded the spring peepers (chorus frogs) while under-taking the famous library book burial. It's been twenty-five years since I slept in that house on RR#2, and still the shrill sound of spring peepers can take me back there in an instant. Only the male frogs of this species make the high-pitched "peep" to attract mates (and me). Wikipedia describes them best: "As a chorus, they re-semble the sounds of sleigh bells." If I had to pick a sound of home, a sound that identified and solidified nearly twenty years, it would be the peepers.

And Kiley's screams. Our dog Xanadu's nails on the steel front door as he begged to come in even though he had just been let out. The familiar twang of that stupid wheat-sheaf table as a piece of metal wheat coiled back and pierced a body part. The soundtrack would also include Party Line Grandma's rolling cough, which alerted us to her pending arrival as she crossed the two acres from her house to ours.

There were also the two sounds synonymous with my grand-father (besides the blaring radio stock-market report on hog prices): the whirr of his snowmobile as it raced across the fields to our house and the sound of the irrigation pipes being connected in the tobacco rows across from us in the summer. "Get your swim-suits on! They're irrigating!"

And, of course, the harsh-impact *thwack* of the Cabbage Patch Kid connecting with my head. Yes, the sounds of home.

5.
High School (Not So) Confidential

DISCLOSURE: CAROLE POPE of Rough Trade would have been on my Top Ten you-know-what list if I'd been aware of her at the time.

Actual soundtrack: my Ray Lynch cassette tape *Deep Breakfast*, a trippy New Age electro album. I bought it because of the J-card that read: "Evelyn slapped Raymond on the back with a laugh. 'You must be starved, old friend. Come into my apartment, and we'll suffer through a deep breakfast of pure sunlight.'" Increasingly, my soundtrack was drowned out by my sister's mauve boom box and her high school anthem, "Mr. Jones" by Counting Crows. It was her get-up-and-go.

Kiley, Dax and I had all catapulted into our teen years at various stages and were all equally adamant about our needs. We wanted the teen basics: a phone, TV and potato chips. Dax would sub in the Internet and his desire to be on the computer 24-7, back in the days of dial-up, and this foiled any opportunities for Kiley and me to have phone conversations.

Kiley wanted to talk on the phone all the time because she had just read the book *Being Your Best: Tina Yothers' Guide for Girls*. Tina was famous for her role as Jennifer Keaton on the TV series *Family Ties*, and she was Kiley's role model. While Tina provided "advice for teenage and preteen girls on friendship, school and family life, health and beauty and fashion, and other subjects," Kiley did the same, on the phone, for hours. In a move fuelled by pure exasperation, Kiley had her own private line installed so she could have more time to share her beauty and fashion wisdom with her circle of friends (former White Rabbit Club members). She had to finance this herself, as my parents didn't feel this was a necessity item. Kiley took on several jobs to pay for the precious phone, and my parents ended up taking on an unexpected part-time job themselves: driving Kiley around to all her jobs.

I was into my phone phase too. I wanted to chat to the pals I'd met at summer art camp. I'd finally found "my people" and suffered from being incommunicado when my kid bro discovered online chat rooms. My people had purple hair and screen-printed their own T-shirt designs. They wore entire sets of cutlery as bangles on their wrists and didn't go anywhere without an old Pentax camera around their necks or a small sketchbook shoved into their back pockets. This tribe was eccentric, colourful and unlike any I had encountered. It was a herd of united zaniness that I wanted to run wild with.

I also entered my vegetarian phase at seventeen. I decided to be an angsty teen and join the vibrant vegetarian movement, because I liked tie-dye T-shirts, beeswax candles, planting trees and listening to Ani DiFranco. Exploratory vegetarianism was an integral part of this curriculum.

My parents were receptive, but my mother was realistic. She wasn't a short-order cook, and she wasn't prepared to redesign mealtime around my whims. My red-meat sabbatical involved a lot of chickpeas, specifically crappy chickpea burgers that I voluntarily made. They were hockey pucks of mashed chickpeas and crushed garlic cloves—I haven't had a cold since—that crumbled and fell out of the bun with the first bite. When I didn't make chickpea burgers for my exquisite vegetarian meal of the day, I had potato chips, usually plain ones enhanced with dashes of red-wine vinegar (because my siblings and I would make quick work of the dill pickle or sour cream and onion chips in one sitting, and "grocery night" was but one night a week—Thursdays).

Like typical teens, Kiley, Dax and I were all on our own emotional missions. We gathered when we had to for dinner, but as we underwent metamorphosis, we wanted to be cocooned in our own rooms on the phone. Or, in Dax's case, in Internet chat rooms or the weight room.

By high school, Dax had achieved superhuman strength from his strict weightlifting regime. He did this in the morning, before school, when Kiley and I had our own battles going on. I'd like to say his muscles came from a combination of weightlifting, a steady after-school diet that consisted of three buttered kaiser buns (butter spread as thick as cake icing) and homemade banana splits, and couch hauling. Dax would regularly haul both Kiley and me off the coveted end of the couch, the one closest to the TV.

Next to Dr. Ruth's radio show, TV featured large in our semi-sheltered country lives for its real-world curriculum. The only two programming choices my siblings and I agreed upon were a healthy balance of education and inappropriateness: *Degrassi Junior High* and *Porky's. Degrassi* was usually on after school, while *Porky's* was a late, late night affair on CityTV. While it was an iffy channel for reception, it carried reliably racy movies with boobs and suggestive sex scenes. When the news broadcast came on, the newscaster would say, "It's eleven o'clock; do you know where your children are?" We were downstairs licking the salt and vinegar flavouring off our bowls of chips and watching *Porky's*! We huddled around the TV like it was a campfire, because there was no door to the basement and the volume had to be kept to mouse level. This was when we really got along as siblings. Like a Norman Rockwell painting, right?

Despite my growing celeb crush list, the real world failed to produce any action like the *Degrassi* scripts suggested. Was I destined to be a celebrity stalker? I seemed to be on cruise control in high school and wondered if maybe Tina Yothers's boob exercises *were* the solution. I had dalliances with boys in high school, don't get me wrong—but it only took one foggy Black Label encounter with a long-haired guy doused in Drakkar Noir to confirm that I was content to wait. We didn't go "all the way," but far enough along the way for me to recognize that this was exactly what Dr. Ruth was talking about.

Even after that clarifying Black Label encounter, I went to prom with a boy—was it a big bluff? I don't remember this being a conscious move, i.e., "Surely they won't think I'm gay if I go to the senior prom with Mark Picketts." He was your typical hunky athletic guy with shaggy blond hair, braces and weight-room bulked muscles. I didn't fool his mother, though. I was informed by a family friend that she reported to her high-society tea circle: "Julie Torti wore a pantsuit to the prom!" My parents didn't care that I wore a pantsuit (though my mom was heavily concerned about my decision to wear white sweat socks instead of black dress *chaussettes*).

There was definitely gay talk floating around—but not about me, even me in my pantsuit. I recall the time when, as clear as day in the freshly fallen snow and in full 180-degree view of the school's library windows, a small group had stamped out ANITA LIKES PUSSY. A bunch of football players were blamed for outing her. Maybe she did like pussy, maybe she didn't; it was the stuff of high school.

Brantford Collegiate Institute wasn't numb to the presence of gays. Sandy, a really effeminate guy with a matching lisp, was constantly stuffed into lockers. Billie Jo, who I would have pegged as "liking pussy," was as tough as Tonya Harding. Her serious butch presence in the school smoking area was revered. I questioned Billie Jo's tendencies when she sent me a folded note via "her people" indicating that she wanted to beat the shit out of me for dancing with Mike Penczak at the prom. I was supposed to meet her in the smoking area that afternoon after school. But I had a bus to catch and I let it be known that Billie Jo could have Mike. Or Anita for that matter. No need to go all *Fight Club*. She was acting like it was the final *Dirty Dancing* scene at Kellerman's Resort. And I hadn't exactly been having the time of my life with Mike.

I continued believing that I was a fabulous interloper and hung out exclusively with a pack of guys who horsed around, wrestled in public places and lit their jeans on fire with Zippo lighter fluid. They smoked unfiltered Camels, screeched doughnut marks into the pavement of any empty parking lot and played guitars. We found rope swings along the river and skinny-dipped, ate cheap tacos from Taco Bell and listened to the Doors and Neil Young. I don't remember talking about boyfriends or girlfriends or even worrying about not being with someone. We drank Upper Canada lager and watched Quentin Tarantino films, trying to fast-forward our way through the school year. Collectively, we couldn't wait to press Play on our own future episodes or at least get to summer break.

I graduated from camper to counsellor at the Scarborough Visual Arts Camp on Red Pine Lake in Haliburton, Ontario. I asked to be the counsellor in charge of the journalism program and would oversee the production of the daily *Camp Log* newspaper. I'd be working directly with Claire, who I knew from afar, and even though she wasn't a celeb, she had a place on my Top Ten list. Everyone else at camp was pining for the buff kayak instructor, *Tim.* You had to say his name in italics. He was undeniably cute, with his sly smile and biceps pumped as he hoisted kayaks over his head as if they were weightless, but my affections were captured by Claire. I knew something kinetic was happening, because my blood would feel too hot for my veins when she was around. And as the official journalism instructor, Claire was around a lot. How convenient that I could be the counsellor assigned to the journalism program. She reminded me of one of the *Sweet Valley High* twins, all grown up and world-wise. (Kiley read the series; I only knew the twins from the books' paperback covers.) Claire's skin smelled like Skin So Soft (Avon's pleasantly scented mosquito repellent). Her hair was just like Barbie's—straight, cornsilk blond and brushed into a sheen that made me want to learn how to braid hair. Naturally, Claire was the tennis instructor as well. *Tim* had muscles but they seemed too jacked up—like Popeye's. Claire pulled muscles off with more grace, and I enjoyed sitting courtside, perfecting her portrait in charcoal for the camp drawing class as she bounced balls and pounded them over the net again and again.

Because the camp was organized by the Scarborough Board of Education, all the campers and staff were from the Toronto area—except me. They say friends are priceless, but Flo could tell you exactly how much such friendships cost. While Dax ate up the dial-up, I learned that I could squeeze in conversations (and any remaining chips) during his weightlifting routine. Come September, the phone bill at RR#2 spiked dramatically due to my new arty circle. I couldn't pick enough pine cones out of the forest to finance my chatting, so I was forced to sell items of clothing to Kiley. This was actually an ideal transaction, as I could still "steal" back the purchased items and wear them to school on the days I knew she was at a soccer tournament or science field trip. We had a few public fisticuffs in the high school hallways when Kiley spotted me strutting past in "her" clothes.

My mom will deny this story forever, but this is when the term "fuckshit" was coined in the family. It was 8:15 a.m., and Kiley and I were in the house, not outside at the end of the driveway where we should have been to catch the bus. My poor mother, also readying herself for work, came around the corner into her daughters' spitting match. I took off in Kiley's shoes. "Stop your GD swearing and get your lunches!" ("GD" was "goddamn" in polite-speak in our house.) She cut through the living room to the front door and handed me something warm in foil for my breakfast to go. (I know, how spoiled was I?) I asked her what was in the foil. My mom, in utter frustration, said, "It's a piece of fuckshit!" Well, you can imagine the laughter. *Fuckshit?* I ran out of the house with my foil-wrapped fuckshit and got on the bus, with Kiley punching my back. Happy, golden memories of the teen years, indeed. What would Tina Yothers say about that?

This is partly why summer camp was such a peaceful retreat, but I also had a squeaky new identity and an ever-evolving persona at camp. Most kids thought it sucked to be shuffled off to a sleepover camp for the summer, but I was in my element. I fancied myself as having the same mysterious allure as the new kid in class. (To this day, this also largely explains my continued non-stop travels: I can be the "new person" everywhere, every single day.)

I became "campsick," never homesick, and my long-distance phone bills were indicative of this. I shifted to the art of pen-palling when monthly phone payments were eating up my wage from the nature centre, where I led snow-panted Girl Guides on owl prowls and seniors on wildflower walks. I holed up in my room and wrote mile-long letters on foolscap to nearly forty friends at one point. I still have all the letters they sent in return. Claire and I wrote back and forth, with the fever of a tennis match (the fever being one-sided, of course). I didn't have the guts to actually call her—besides, she had moved to Albuquerque, New Mexico, to pursue university studies. She once sent me an image of a lizard that was found in a nearby cave from around 10,000 BCE. This cave art drawing would become my first tattoo—sitting just inside my left hip. Chameleons can blend and adapt to their surroundings, or do the complete opposite. This was me, or what I desired to be. I sought out Dave at Tattoo U near my high school, and while he ate a double-patty hamburger from Admiral's, he inked me for good. For fifty dollars, this was the best thing I'd bought in life so far.

Despite being temporarily grounded for getting a tattoo (groundings never had any long-lasting enforcement in our house), I took over my parents' old purple bedroom (walls, carpet, duvet) and did a rapid redo, starting with an undo of the purple. I set about recreating summer camp in my bedroom. I applied landscape wallpaper of a misty pine forest, the kind of decor commonly seen in a dentist's office in the 1980s. I wanted to bring the outdoors in— and this was way before rustic chic was a thing. I had a real poplar tree trunk that went from floor to ceiling. The trunk had a birdhouse nailed to it and a genuine wasp nest dangling from a branch by fishing line. On that same branch I hung a pipe cleaner bumblebee mobile. In front of the wall with the forest mural, I plugged in a faux fireplace. Just the logs—the kind that looks like a primitive campfire, with a rolling mechanism inside to create the flicker. For authenticity, I collected a dozen stones to circle my firepit. On the ceiling, I replicated the northern sky at night with glow-in-the-dark stars. Orion's Belt. Betelgeuse. Sirius. I was three constellations short of a Kumbaya.

As long as I was living at RR#2, I wanted to be ensconced in my reverie, and my reverie was camp. The same summer I was a newbie journalism counsellor at Camp Walden's art camp, I was selected for Bark Lake's outdoor leadership camp, even farther north from everything familiar. Just as art camp illuminated my winters, Bark Lake added to this same reassuring glow of belonging when I met Sharon. And, in turn, she introduced me to the Indigo Girls.

It was a sluggish night in August, and our group was gathered around the lake's edge after a day of portaging and leaping off Jumper's Rock. The fire was snapping, and stars were falling out of the sky by the dozen. It was showtime for the Perseids meteor showers. Sharon strummed her guitar and sang "Closer to Fine" into the stillness of the night. We collectively held our breath—her voice was ethereal, and she was singing words that made so much sense to our teenaged brains. I hadn't even heard of the Indigo Girls. (I would later learn that the Indigo Girls were my people too, in more ways than one.)

Back then, I'm sure the expression was, "Sharon's the bomb." But to me—she was the balm. She fell somewhere between a crush and a mentor to me—someone I wanted to impress and a woman whose presence made my palms clammy. She was so confident, whether it was handling a canoe, a guitar or a tweaked trapezius muscle. She listened with such intensity, her pistachio-green eyes locked on mine. Sharon was straight, but I enjoyed how she made my core temperature rise. She was also a shiatsu instructor—something I'd never heard of. I liked that she could communicate in so many ways, through song and touch. She gave me her sun-faded baseball hat that had "Bark Lake" stitched on the front and her name in smaller font on the back. I felt like a cheerleader who'd just been handed the star quarterback's leather varsity jacket to keep her warm at the drive-in. I wore that silly hat like those cheerleaders wore their boys' jackets.

At Bark Lake I found more tribe members. I gravitated early on to a tall, lanky guy from Warkworth, Ontario, named Antoine. He was a captivating raconteur. His dad did photography for *National Geographic*, and I wondered if I'd seen his stuff years before, curled up in Nan's library with a Tahiti Treat. His mom made bread from scratch every day, with flour she had delivered to her from a mill in Saskatchewan. And they still had an outhouse! Antoine was a prolific writer and so well-read that most of the time I didn't even know who he was quoting, but he was intriguing and cerebral. His older brother Georg lived in Toronto, and surprisingly, my parents let me take the train into the city to meet Antoine and Georg for the day.

Antoine was at home in both the city and the country—and had no qualms about spinning about the downtown streets on his dad's folding bicycle. I followed behind on Georg's too-tall mountain bike, hoping to not be creamed by a streetcar. We made a beeline for Chinatown, somewhere I had only passed by in a car with my parents. We rarely went to downtown Toronto (except for the Royal Ontario Museum), instead clinging to the outskirts for zoo visits and the Canadian National Exhibition. Antoine and I poked around the market stalls, buying odd little things like dried seahorses (I made a necklace out of mine, threading leather between its curled tail) and ginger candies. We hatched a plan that day: we were going to move to Australia after high school and my final year of summer camp. Antoine had it all figured out, and his conviction fish-hooked me.

"After high school" came sooner for me than for Antoine—
I quit five days before I would have graduated (which, to me,
shouldn't be considered quitting at all). I wasn't overly concerned
that this would interfere with my future, as my horizon never
really indicated university. I had my own version of post-secondary
education to tend to and was confident that my schooling would
unfold like the drumbeats in the 1963 Surfaris hit "Wipe Out."
Before my scheme with Antoine, I had planned to:

- Tag sea turtles off the coast of Georgia
- Plant trees in California with an organization called
  Peace Trees
- Walk across Canada (not for a cause or anything,
  just for something to do and experience)
- Clean birds after tragic oil spills
- Become a self-proclaimed ornithologist in the Galapagos,
  discovering something that Darwin didn't
- Live in the Yukon (meaningful work to be determined)

I thought my curriculum was better curated than the standard
post-secondary offerings presented to me. I had been identified as
gifted in elementary school, and the education officials were not
impressed that I was giving up on my gifts. In my last year of high
school, when I was supposed to be crushing deadlines and pulling
all-nighters to nab a coveted 98.9 percent average and Top Student
in Brant County designation, I couldn't care less. I had missed more
than sixty days of school in my final year—but they were well spent.
I was a member of every team: soccer, volleyball, cross-country
running, track. I was part of the Century Running Club and the
yearbook club, and VP of the environment group. My high school

counsellor cited "external pressures" as the reason for my failure to graduate, but she didn't elaborate. Was she really trying to peg this on me being gay? I was bored, yes. Coincidentally bored and gay? Well, yes to that too.

But here's the main reason why I quit high school: I had to get to art camp. I had Claire's Skin So Soft indelibly etched into my hippocampus. I had attended camp every June since grade nine, and although it always conflicted with the final exams, normally I was allowed to write my exams in advance and then take off to camp. Not in my final year, though; when I missed those sixty-plus days, this privilege was revoked. I was told by the vice-principal that I would not be allowed to write exams early, and therefore I wouldn't be allowed to attend art camp either. This meant, logically, that I had to quit school in order to attend camp. (See how gifted I am? This decision made perfect sense to me.)

So, when Antoine introduced his concrete plan to move to Australia, I capitalized on it instantly because I thought it would make an excellent addition to my post-secondary curriculum. He had a lot of the fine print worked out: we could stay with his brother Georg until we found a place and learned how to bake bread. As much as I loved bread, I'd never baked it, but I loved the idea of being on the other side of the globe in the fabled land that I'd known only from *National Geographic*, nature documentaries and *Crocodile Dundee*.

To fund this dream, I decided that we'd make and sell stuff in our backyards and maybe at craft sales. We could spend the summer amassing inventory (beeswax candles, tie-dye shirts and stars that Antoine made out of a super-thin wood-fibre material). I would paint colourful flowerpots ("Hippoflowerpotamuses") and tie-dye long johns ("LongJulies").

Warkworth was 265 kilometres from Mount Pleasant, but somehow Antoine and I (both without driver's licences) managed to see each other—and not in a romantic way, for either of us. He was a *GQ* gorgeous guy, but I was into girls. We were simply attracted to each other's brains and humour. He had a goofy laugh that would contagiously loop in anyone within hearing distance, and then he'd talk seriously about political stuff and literature like a tenured prof. Maybe our parents were crossing their fingers that we had "connected" in other ways, but they never let on. Antoine listened to all sorts of crazy music thanks to his brother's influence. We made cassettes for each other. I had a recording that Sharon mailed to me of her Indigo Girls covers, and I copied that for him, hoping to impress him with my alternative choice. We went together to see They Might Be Giants at the Danforth Music Hall.

One weekend I made the pilgrimage to Warkworth. At Antoine's parents' house, we had sophisticated lunches of chilled cucumber soups and a nip of mead at dinner. Antoine's dad made the mead (honey wine) and honey too—this is how Antoine had a direct beeswax source for candle making. We laid wicks and talked politics (them, not

At this time, I entertained ideas of going to the Yukon as well. I longed to be somewhere that would require a two-day canoe paddle from mail service. I had latched on to the idea of the Yukon after buying a copy of *Another Lost Whole Moose Catalogue*. I was harbouring back-to-the-land fantasies and fancied myself a little log shelter with a tidy garden plot (where I could grow garlic for my vampire-killing I'm-a-vegetarian chickpea burgers and some cherry tomatoes—Dax could sell me some seeds). *Another Lost Whole Moose Catalogue* was patched together by a group of bush hippies. It covered essentials like how to gut a salmon and build an eight-sided log home. It included an edible-wild guide (shaggymane mushrooms, puffballs), tips on beekeeping, pickup truck specs and lots of stuff on sled dogs and making your own rosehip tea. I loved it all. I could pack lightly and survive with this catalogue alone while writing about my own fish-gutting and puffballing adventures.

▶ And there were gays there, too, as I found out by reading the article on page 104: "Yukon Gays: Ending the Isolation." I had even gone so far as to copy out the suggested contact for *Rites*, a Canadian gay news magazine based out of Toronto. I noted further that I was to read anything written by Jane Rule and/or Armistead Maupin to increase my gayness. I decided then that finding the gays on Davie Street in Vancouver would prove to be easier. Apparently, I had a few books to read first too, before I ventured off anywhere. And some publishing credits would definitely help with my fantasy writing job in parts unknown. •

me), and I marvelled at what a cool existence they had. No TV, a bazillion books, clothes hung on the line, honey at the ready and an outhouse! To this day, it's one of the best toilet seat views I've ever had, overlooking the rolling Trent Hills landscape. Antoine and I tie-dyed several dozen T-shirts that weekend, his mother cringing at all the precious well water used in the process.

Antoine was reliable in the sense that everything he exposed me to was marvellous and inspiring. But I backed out of the Australia plan on a whim, as though it were as simple as cancelling a dentist appointment. I remember clinging to the rotary phone handset and the sound of Antoine's voice. It was a dream that was evaporating for no good reason. My dad happily handled cancelling the one-way Qantas plane ticket—that much I remember, but everything else has become unfortunately gauzy. I imagine I cried a lot and then slept a long while over the collapse of my next sure thing. Did I back out because I was scared? Were my parents projecting their fears on me?

I just wasn't ready to jump countries and move a dozen time zones to Australia with Antoine. I didn't want to backpack around Europe or go to university like everyone else had planned—so, if I wasn't going to Australia to bake bread, what the hell was I going to do? Was Australia one of those puzzle pieces that I attempted to jam in, confident that it would fit close enough? I awoke each day imagining for a long while what my Australian bread baker life would have looked like.

I kept track of Antoine, and we hooked up again in Vancouver ten years later when he was home to visit his parents, who had moved to Vancouver Island. He had been in Germany for a bit and was really into the electronic music scene. He did go to Melbourne and open a bakery with his brother, like he said he would. He and Georg sold their bakery, called Loafer, in 2007; they had established themselves as baking superstars. All those dipped beeswax candles. All those dainty stars.

While Antoine made an early start on his career trajectory and followed through on his vision, I was at home with a bunch of tie-dyed long johns and flowerpots. The only shiny spot was my occasional dog-sitting gig in Napanee, Ontario, for Marta, another Bark Lake counsellor. Marta had two affable huskies named after northern lakes (Nakina and Kennisis) and a fabulous art studio in a century-old house by the Napanee River. Her studio was an eclectic showcase of half-finished work, watercolours, polished bones, feathers, well-loved brushes and charcoal smudges. I wanted to live in her studio. Marta's husband, Dave, could play anything on the guitar and had written and performed stuff for *Sesame Street* and CBC's *Mr. Dressup*. Who gets to do that for a day job? He even produced pop star Avril Lavigne's first recording. Marta and Dave's daughter, Renee, was just a little pipsqueak then, busying herself with drawing, mostly unicorns. Their house was a hotbed of dreaming, doodling and magic.

When I'd met Marta at Bark Lake, she was teaching art classes at Queen's University and the Haliburton School of the Arts. She sent me stunning cards of serene winter scenes that she had sketched. This was her job—to draw! She illustrated for *Harrowsmith* magazine and *The Canadian Encyclopedia*. I bought copies of her

Up North wilderness guides, so proud to know the person behind the delicate sketches of flora and fauna. I still have the leather talisman that Marta made at camp that summer, filled with secrets from the earth and sky. It had been an impromptu rainy-day workshop held on an afternoon too soggy to paddle. We were instructed to stitch together a secret talisman with items from the earth, sky, water and something from ourselves, which represented the fire. It would be the mysterious and cosmic combination of these four forces that would bring us good luck—or luck to the person with whom we chose to share it. Marta's was so much more polished than our crude efforts (especially the pocket sewing bit). Her artistic hands turned leather into something to be displayed in a gallery, while the rest of us inexpertly patched together our talismans with chunky beads and sloppy knots. When she tucked her talisman in my palm, I felt that surge of luck and belonging.

With my cave art lizard tattoo, Marta's fire around my neck and the cassette tape of Indigo Girls cover songs from Sharon, I felt invincible. Ready for something. If I wasn't going to bake bread in Australia, then I was going to draw for a magazine, like Marta did. She was the one who tipped me off to the notion that you could do what you love and get paid for it. And do it from home wearing ripped jeans and tie-dyed long johns, not in some starchy office with a dress code and a 9:00 a.m. punch clock.

Like the chameleon inked on my skin, I was adapting. I had blended in for enough years and was now prepared to strike out and become a legit journalist and illustrator, with no previous experience. I was free to a good home.

New plan: land semi-gainful employment at *Cockroach* magazine in Vancouver, BC.

6.

Dumpster Diving: Vancouver

Cockroach, A PUBLICATION by the Environmental Youth Alliance (EYA), meshed with my ripped jeans, nose ring and cassette collection. I had picked up a copy of the newsprint mag at an environmental conference sponsored by EYA in Ottawa a year before and kept it filed away in my drawer of random possibility ideas. David Suzuki headlined the conference and shared the stage with a total blast from the "Baby Beluga" past, Raffi. Milling around the conference before Suzuki spoke, I began chatting with a striking woman wearing colourful beads and feathers in her hair. Beth explained that she was accompanying her friend, a Swiss environmental activist (Bruno Manser), and Mutang, a native of the Penan tribe in Sarawak, Malaysia. Bruno and Mutang later presented a heated talk about the palm oil industry, deforestation, acid rain and climate change—even then, in 1991. Members of the EYA discussed upcoming trips for students into the Costa Rican jungle that encouraged solution-seeking and self-empowerment. I was caught up in the fever of it all, but unsure of where my fit was at the time. Beth's contagious energy prompted me to exchange addresses with her.

Lying on my waterbed one night, under the branches of the tree that I had stuck in the corner of my room, I thought of Beth and started writing her a letter. Beth's world fascinated and intimidated me; from her involvement in theatre to journalism to documentary production, she was living large. She was a rock 'n' roll columnist for a Japanese newspaper and spoke about uranium mining and the Kyoto Protocol. She casually mentioned things, people and places that I had to research (Google wasn't invented yet) and penned me letters from Kyoto that read like poetry. She wrote about stuff like civil disobedience and political unrest, NGOs and timber blockades. She sent me tiny feathers and pressed flowers from Japan, all the while enlightening my little waterbed world of whimsy. She was working as a writer too, and she was proof, like Marta, that you could do what you love and have someone pay you to do it. Shortly after the conference in Ottawa, she landed a gig as David Suzuki's translator in Japan.

With this in mind, I cold-called *Cockroach*. Or cold-wrote them, I suppose, on the back of an old math test that belonged to Dax. They'd appreciate the recycled paper and Dax's high marks. In the letter, I attempted to convince Sam Roddick, the founder and editor of the magazine, that I was the very best candidate for a job that didn't even exist. She was the pioneering daughter of Anita Roddick of the Body Shop franchise fame.

I'd had sugar plum visions of being on the West Coast in high school. My closest pals, Sally and Charlotte, were supposed to come too. It wasn't a definitive plan like the one Antoine and I had sketched out—more of a daydream (and its lifespan was about a day long). I don't know what we thought we'd all do once we had an apartment and Vancouver at our feet, but I kept my eye on Vancouver, and after happening upon a late-night documentary, *Hookers on Davie Street*, I was sold. I had no intention of being a hooker, but I had seen gay people—a lot of them—in this documentary. Particularly on Davie Street. It would be one of the very first streets I would beeline to. I knew this much: I wanted to be gay and away. (If, for some strange reason, you just started reading *Free to a Good Home* and began here, you may have pegged me in an instant. *Cockroach* magazine might not register, but if I talked about heading to Davie Street, then you'd know.)

I hadn't seen many gay people in Brantford, aside from a few token short-haired, whistle-wearing, track-suited phys. ed. teachers at soccer tournaments, and none of them taught at our high school. Our PE teachers were very married, to men. My crush/mentor leanings for beautiful women like Claire and Sharon grew legs seemingly overnight. Even though they weren't gay, my attraction to them was groundwork for my beginner lesbian licence. Besides k.d. lang, the only other gays in Canada seemed to be on Davie Street. High school was now over. I had entered the real world that everyone had cautioned me about and was about to make my mark.

I planned to go to Vancouver and be a writer. My only genuine published work was *Camp Log*, some high school yearbook illustrations and several poetry submissions (featuring my stuffed animals) with the Junior Reporter Club of the *Brantford Expositor*. But the *Brantford Expositor* and Brantford in general were too mainstream for my eighteen-year-old self.

In Vancouver, Sam Roddick had assembled an eco-warrior crew of hack writers to cover stories on anti-establishment actions, the bear bile industry and all things granola. I wanted in. I wanted to write for the magazine, for free even. I sent her an intense five-page letter about how cool I was and promised to be so flexible that I'd sleep on any couch provided and live on Pop-Tarts. As far as Sam and the *Cockroach* team were concerned, I could have submitted a Swiss Chalet menu instead of a high school diploma.

I couldn't wait to be immersed in gayness (once I increased my own personal level by reading Jane Rule) and to have the distance and identity newness that sacred places like art camp and Bark Lake had provided me.

The same week I sent my secret job application (and job creation) letter to Sam, my mom gave me a well-loved copy of *How to Live on Nothing* by Joan Shortney. I suppose my lack of a practical career-focused future was an indicator for my parents of what was to come. The book illustrated how to darn socks and make cakes over a fire in a halved grapefruit peel. Sensing my transparent need for independence, my mom suggested that I build a little cabin on the edge of our property by the tracks. "Build yourself a little shed or tree house, live out there, and think about things." But I was set on Vancouver and Davie Street. (Work ideas, I'll be honest, were purely secondary to finding a girlfriend.)

I finally had some momentum in some direction—with intention even. A job prospect, maybe. I reread the letters from Sharon, Beth and Marta that shared snippets of their successfully creative lives. I could sense energy particles from their force fields clinging to me. Vancouver seemed plausible and about the only thing that made my heart pound with enthusiasm.

My parents had one stiff stipulation: I had to have a thousand dollars in my bank account. In 1992 this was like a million dollars. Especially because I only worked weekends at the nature centre for $5.25 an hour and at a canoe company for a few hours for even less.

I didn't hear back from Sam immediately, but I held strong to my West Coast dreams. It was actually Daniel, one of the editors at

Cockroach, who wrote back (on my original letter, in giant scrawl). It was brief, but he confirmed that Sam shared my enthusiasm and he was certain they could find a spot for me at the magazine. "Heck, I'll put you up at my place; you can sleep on the couch." They couldn't believe I would work for free, and they thought maybe they could find some money for me in time. That was about it. I didn't show this particular job acceptance letter to my parents (because if I did, I might still be living with them), but it was all I needed to catapult myself out of the province as soon as my thousand-dollar goal was reached.

I painted some wall murals at my high school and the bedroom of a math teacher's son. I painted tropical fish in Dax's modified gym in our basement for a handsome payout (by my parents, not Dax) and topped up my savings account with a more lucrative job painting the store sign for Brantford's only indie coffee shop at the time, the Red Rocket Café. I expanded my production line to batik shirts and incense holders made out of Das air-dry modelling clay. I had patched together just enough money to finance my western pilgrimage. My life's soundtrack was updated to "Go West" by the Pet Shop Boys.

I was ready to strike out and leave everything that was familiar to me and find that elusive *we*. I had my one thousand dollars, a musty Canadian Tire sleeping bag, a sketchbook, my Halley's Comet Swatch watch, friendship bracelets up to my elbow, all my trusty pen pal addresses and my favourite cassette tapes (Jane Siberry, Ani DiFranco and Sharon's Indigo Girls covers). I was on top of the world. I had a job lined up at *Cockroach*, writing a column about important things, a couch and a place to stay in a place I'd never been to. My parents pressed for more details as my departure date grew closer, but I didn't have any to offer. I was confident that this plan was foolproof.

That's why this fool got off the airport bus as soon as she saw the West Twenty-Seventh intersection in Vancouver. I was unaware that Daniel's house was nearly four kilometres west of the Granville Street intersection where the bus dropped me. It was August, and I had worn all my "heavy stuff" on the flight, as per my mom's recommendations, to free up space in my backpack. I had on my winter hiking boots with wool socks, my power jeans (Levi's with the button-fly flap cut off to reveal the buttons) with a few safety pins up the hem (a nineties trend, not a budget hem), Marta's mighty talisman around my neck (along with a pound of other leather necklaces bearing teeth and beads) and a Beaver Canoe hooded sweatshirt. Very Vancouver. Very hot.

I walked and walked with the weight of *my* world on my back. First observation: For every road in Vancouver there is a back alley—and for every back alley, there are bushes and bushes of giant thimble-sized blackberries. Free.

At Carnarvon and Twenty-Seventh, with the Beaver Canoe hoodie knotted around my waist and a big backpack sweat patch on my T-shirt, I knocked on the door of my new home. I breathed it all in—cedar trees and the clarity of that mountain and ocean air commingling in the Georgia Strait. This was it!

Nobody answered, but a dog barked back. I went to the back of the house, charged on the adrenalin of the day. I had started off in Brantford and was now in Vancouver, eating blackberries from the alleys. I knocked a lot on a few doors and double-checked the address. Eventually, a woman entered the backyard with her son. She asked who I was waiting for, and I proudly told her I wasn't really waiting for anyone; I was going to live there. As soon as someone let me in. She offered me a Coke and assured me that someone would be home soon. "There's a whole pile of them that live upstairs. Shannon works at the bank and is usually home by five."

I had no idea who Shannon was. In my sparse job confirmation letter from Daniel, there was no explanation of anything. "Bring your bike and some money. We'll show you the best spots for dumpster diving." Dumpster diving? I would have to patiently wait to find out what this meant. I had Daniel's home address (which was apparently also Shannon's) and a phone number that he failed to answer.

When Shannon arrived home later that afternoon, I had already set up a comfortable backyard base camp. I busied myself with *real world* curricula, reading the essential *Catcher in the Rye*. Shannon didn't know anything about my arrival. She was skeptical and asked what the arrangement was with Daniel—How long was I staying? Did I have furniture?—because there was no room. Where was I supposed to be sleeping? Daniel was already sleeping with two people in his room, in one bed.

I had a lot to learn about bohemia.

Shannon proved to be the most level-headed of the lot and had seen so many roommates come and go since she had moved into West Twenty-Seventh from a tiny reserve in Saskatchewan. Everyone was transient and from somewhere else—my story wasn't new or remarkable. Liz and Daniel were from Ottawa. "Toumbi" was Ontario stock too. Reluctantly, Shannon invited me in. "Daniel didn't mention you, sorry." I found my place on the couch, and Shannon asked if I wanted fruit salad for dinner. We cut grapes and bananas together and split some vanilla yogurt. There was a jumble of furniture and milk crates and no TV. Shannon's room seemed the most established with a wall of Kate Moss Calvin Klein ads and a futon bed. The house, built in the 1930s, had seen a lot of reckless renters in its day. I wasn't being picky, but the grass was overgrown, the hedges needed attention, the deck was ready to collapse and the interior of the house was a dated hodgepodge. Coming from RR#2, it was my first smack of reality. This is what *Living on Nothing* would get me.

The most notable "furnishing" in the house was Daniel's six-foot-tall papier mâché penis. It was still a work in progress, the chicken-wire frame almost completely covered in newspaper strips. Shannon rolled her eyes. "I *really* hate that thing." It took up half the living room.

When I asked about Daniel's whereabouts, she said he'd gone off with Toumbi two weeks ago. They were riding their bikes to Vancouver Island, to Clayoquot Sound, to protest the logging giants. Getting to Clayoquot via the Pacific Rim Highway entailed an 850-kilometre ride. Shannon didn't seem impressed or interested. "I have no idea when he'll be back, but he will be, sometime."

It was almost ten days later when Daniel and Toumbi returned, weathered and covered in chain grease and sweat. They each wore a foot of a raven on a string—symbolic of their journey and the dead bird they'd found en route. Daniel had mostly forgotten about his free couch invite and job offer. I was mildly alarmed, but I knew that I could sniff out something in my new wonderland if need be. I had a thousand dollars, after all.

"Do you have a bike?" he asked. I did, but I hadn't brought it with me. My parents said they could ship it out, once I was settled and was sure it was something I wanted. It seemed to be a rite of passage, as the entire back deck of the house was full of bikes in various states, with modified handlebars, neon pegs, mag wheels—all covered in activist stickers. Without a bike of my own, how could I be accepted as a true gang member?

Steven, another roommate from Prince Rupert, rode in behind the guys on his tricked-out BMX. Literally. He rode right inside the house and around the living room and hopped up the stairs on his bike. Shannon told me he apparently did movie stunt work.

Dan, another movie extra whose hands were filmed in a (don't quote me) Joan Rivers movie, ate nothing but bags of boiled perogies. Daniel, Toumbi and Liz took turns shaving each other's heads in various asymmetrical patterns. The styles were right out of *The Last of the Mohicans*. Daniel's hair was as long as Liz's but not as long at Toumbi's, which had braids and beads and feathers woven into it. It was a lot of hair in one bed, that's for sure. There was so much creativity in one house, with the papier mâché penis, Kate Moss collages, BMX stunts and full-time actors! I was inspired. I took a picture of my new roommates to send home. I can only imagine the horror and wonder that was involved as my parents looked at them.

Later that night, as the rain began to spit down, Daniel asked if I was hungry and wanted to join him on a dumpster dive. I had no clue what this diving thing was about, but I said yes, with a squeak. "You can borrow Liz's bike." Liz had a ten-speed and was even taller than me. I rode on my tiptoes, cranking her bike up the steep, slick climb to wherever this dumpster-dive event was. Daniel basically lived on his bike seat and hopped every curb along the way.

We leaned our bikes against a chain-link fence in the darkness behind a Chinese grocery store. Daniel hopped right in the steaming dumpster, saying I wouldn't believe what they found at this place on a regular basis. Whole pineapples with visible dents. Dozens of apples with a few blemishes. Packages of tofu that had just expired that day. Daniel handed me some limp broccoli and a stiff baguette. I soon learned that "dumpster diving" was getting dinner. It was how Daniel and Toumbi and Liz grocery shopped. (Shannon did not partake in this. She had her limits, and a steady income from the bank.)

It had never occurred to me to poke around in a dumpster for food. Why would I? We got our groceries at Calbeck's every

Thursday and our just-baked buns from the bakery in Paris or Burford.

I chalked it all up as bohemia. I wrote my army of pen pals about this new life of mine. Dumpster dinners, the big penis in the living room, riding bikes in the rain and dodging banana slugs as long as my fingers.

I was a real live journalist with ten or eleven roommates, living the dream over candlelit broccoli stir-fry. I wasn't *Living on Nothing*. This was something. It was real.

7.

Bohemian Rhapsody

I HAD WANTED TO LIVE somewhere different, where I didn't know a soul, and I could write about it all. Embracing my dumpster-diving lifestyle, I adopted an appropriate "uniform," giving up on my hippie haute couture. In a nearby dumpster, I found a pair of bleached-out Levi's jeans with a big Budweiser patch sewn in the crotch. Awesome. Shannon gave me one of her old Indian motorcycle T-shirts, and I found a new-to-me pair of nine-hole scuffed army boots. I was as gay as could be.

When I moved to Vancouver, I thought a new address and new province also warranted a new handle. I tried "J.T." on for size. (A high school bud called me this.) Nobody else really picked up on it, but I wanted it to catch. How did k.d. pull it off? In lower case, no less! I was heavily into J.D. Salinger at this point too, so initials were necessary, as I was a writer and making my mark at *Cockroach*. Shannon saw through the transparency of my name immediately. On the first day I met her in the backyard, she said flatly,

"J.T.? What's your real name?" She pressed until I caved, and I was never J.T. again with her. It was a cornball thing to do, but I was really working that Douglas Coupland theory that everything was waiting to be written. Not even rewritten, just written for the first time. *Choose Your Own Adventure*: blank page, not yet numbered.

Shannon proved my fraudulence a few times, not with a mean intention—more so out of her sage experience with strife. When she let me tag along to a sweat lodge with her, it became clear that I was some eighteen-year-old rather privileged schmuck, dumpster diving for fun, sitting in a sweat lodge with a group of women who were faced with real demons, addictions and loss. I was shiny and unscathed. It was a precious moment for me, being invited to that sweat lodge. Shannon would become my "older sister" in a sense—free to tell me where and when I was going wrong and being a dork. On the flip side, she guided me to a place she had already discovered years ago and took me to my first gay bar, the Lotus Club. Shannon introduced me to real live gays, lent me her book of poetry by Chrystos and asked me, kindly, to keep my hand out of my pants while I read it. When I returned it (after two engrossed sessions of reading and extracurricular activity), we exchanged knowing smiles.

I was embarrassed to admit to Shannon, however, that I had sold dream catchers in high school as part of a fundraiser for a Native Club trip to Albuquerque, New Mexico. When I did eventually confess to the dream catcher fundraiser, she was disappointed in me. She gave me a sharp elbow and a singsong "J.T." whenever I came off as a phony. And selling dream catchers as a white person? Definitely phony.

Still, she introduced me to her pack of friends at the Lotus, a warehouse where they had lesbian dances every Friday. It was like I had to earn my stripes with Shannon, and I was willing.

We drank Okanagan pear ciders and took in the crowd. Although I was taking it all in, in huge gulps, I played it cool with Shannon at my side, and I expressed interest in a woman with kinky hair and a laugh that boomed over the music. She was all muscle; her white T-shirt was tucked into her Levi's and revealed dedication to some kind of physical discipline. Her skin was like coffee with just enough cream. She smoked, which should have been a deterrent, but she could pull it off—and she looked dead sexy exhaling with an eye on the thumping room. Shannon said her name was Cherry and she was a carpenter or something. And Shannon assured me, "She'll never be interested in you. You're just a pup."

Shannon turned her attention to Angelina, a femme she'd been chasing for months, who wore spurs on her cowboy boots. I was left nursing the last of my cider and decided to chat up this Cherry. I said really doorknob things like, "If you married Don Cherry, you'd be Cherry Cherry. Or, if you married right fielder Darryl Strawberry, you'd be Cherry Strawberry." Yeah, pathetic! But Cherry made eye contact, drank her Bud and politely blew smoke over my head.

"You're Shannon's roommate?" she asked me.

"Yeah. Shannon says you'd never sleep with me because I'm just some young pup."

Cherry smiled. "Well, Shannon doesn't know everything."

We obviously talked longer than that, but I have no idea about what. Salt-N-Pepa were drowning out most of our yelled words to each other, which was probably a good thing for me and my conversation starters. Cherry bought me a Bud, and I took that as a good sign. I was ready for anything. Angelina and her spurs left the bar early, Shannon pouted, and I told Shannon I was going home with Cherry, for sure. Shannon didn't believe it (nor did I), but it happened.

In her grass-green Fiat Spider with the top down, Cherry and I cruised through Vancouver's East Side. The September air was clean and electric, but the car was so tiny I felt like there wasn't enough space for my beating heart. Her hand slid between my legs, and I reciprocated. We drank more beer at her house, a spartan rental with creaky wood floors and limited decor. I didn't care— I wasn't there for decor. Her cat Jade had giant chartreuse eyes that followed my every move. Cherry put on groovy mood music, just like they do in the movies (Natalie Merchant, I think?). We picked the labels off of our bottles and shared sloppy kisses, with the cat's tail curling under our chins.

She had been up since six that morning and was ready for the sack. I had been ready for the sack for years! I think I borrowed her toothbrush, or maybe we didn't even bother with teeth brushing at all. Her lips and hips were brushing up against mine instead. Cherry's mattress was on the floor, and our doubly smoky bar clothes were piled in a quick heap. I felt her up and down, bones, skin, kinky hair—it was happening. I had moved from a dormant gay to *Yes I Am!* This was better than a silly high school diploma; I had graduated into a real, practicing lesbian. (I won't expand on the details, because my parents will be reading this and, while I know "they" say "Dance like nobody is watching," you can fill in the dance moves from here.)

Cherry and I didn't become an item. This was okay with me, though; a one-night heavy-petting session fulfilled our needs. After half a dozen beers, sure, we were connected, but I didn't want to be with a smoker on a daily basis. I was undeniably grateful for that one smouldering night, and every time I saw Cherry at the Lotus (where she was a fixture), I'd quiver a little, remembering those bony hips and her experienced tongue. Shannon didn't let me hear the end of it, and I razzed her back about her girl with spurs.

I was authentic now, walking around the Lotus with some chutz-pah. I lived for the weekends and became a fixture myself. During the week, I frequented Little Sister's Book & Art Emporium (the lesbian bookstore) on Davie, hoping to find a woman or a good book to distract me.

Work at *Cockroach* didn't exactly fill my days. I had two assigned stories to research, one of which involved collaboration with Severn Suzuki, David Suzuki's daughter. It was an article on body image and eating disorders, and I needed Barbie dolls for photos. Enter Severn. She was the only kid any of us knew who had a Barbie collection we could use for photo ops. (My Spirograph moment here was interviewing her dad for *Harrowsmith* magazine in Toronto twenty-four years later and recounting this Barbie connection to Dr. Suzuki during my hurried fifteen-minute time slot with him at his downtown institute.)

My other groundbreaking *Cockroach* story was on the bear bile industry and underground Asian markets for such aphrodisiacs. Big, weighty stuff. I'd spent a few weeks sitting around the *Cockroach* headquarters, mostly starry-eyed that it was all happening. This was my life! I was working in Vancouver, as a journalist, just like I said I would. The *Cockroach* office (production, distribution, circulation desk, flop zone) was housed in an old, siding-clad two-storey near the beach, smack dab in the groovy Kitsilano 'hood. I didn't have much of a skill set to offer, beyond writing and doodling. When my idle days moved from starry-eyed enthusiasm to the height of boredom, I announced that I was going to go to the library to conduct research and would report back. Sam shrugged and said I could come and go as I pleased.

En route to the library, I was sidetracked by a lineup for a Vancouver International Film Fest matinee. Research was postponed—hey, I was freelance. Later that day I blew seventy-five dollars on a purple Mountain Equipment Co-op jacket (another Vancouver rite of passage) to endure the soggy days. I was really making it—job, jacket, interest in sophisticated films. When I returned to work the next day, Sam asked if a $350 a month wage was acceptable. I was ecstatic! I had received paycheques before, but this was different. I was doing exactly what I had wanted: I was a struggling writer, sleeping on a couch with a papier mâché penis within reach.

Luckily my parents and grandmothers were sending regular care packages as though I were at summer camp. (Most days, I felt like I was.) The packages contained boxes of tea, tins of International Café powdered coffees—always French Vanilla—and various treats. Sometimes they'd contain a cheque for fifty dollars for a birthday or a twenty-dollar bill. This rounded out my *Cockroach* salary perfectly. Initially. I soon learned that when you earn $350 and your rent is $350 or $425 (because someone didn't pony up or moved out at the last minute), $1,000 is really chump change.

I became keenly aware that while my roommates were also living the dream and pursuing creative lives, they were also flat broke. They shared beds, not just bedrooms, in order to save money. As an employed BMX stunt biker, Steve survived on jars of greasy oolichan from home. (Also known as candlefish, these fish contain so much grease that they can be burned like candles when dried. Regrettably, Steve and I never shared a candlefish-lit dinner.)

A newer roomie, Rick, was on a student budget, with even skinnier cheques from his band council in Stoney Nation, Alberta. He was attending the Emily Carr University of Art and Design, and we somehow ended up sharing a room—mostly because he had a mattress, and I was happy to upgrade from the couch. Trust me—this was a platonic move. Rick was gayer than Liberace. Also sharing our eight-by-eight-foot room were Rick's "kids," Sushi and Cypress. Sushi was the most cross-eyed Siamese I had ever seen. Cypress was a gorgeous longhair who took to sleeping in one of Rick's shoeboxes.

Our house was mostly empty during the day, until the magazine ceased production and I no longer had to report to work by my goal time of noon(ish). I took "Come and go as you please" at face value—and then the magazine itself did the same, after the bank account became empty and there was no new grant money. This was just a few months after I'd started. What followed was an odd, soul-satisfying but suspended time of true unemployment that I viewed as a necessary time for exploration, immersion and research of some sort. My new occupation was walking, all day long. I walked around the verdant University Endowment Lands in woods that sounded like construction sites because of all the pileated woodpecker activity. Everything was triple-sized compared to the boreal forests in Ontario, from the umbrella ferns to the fat banana slugs and mile-high Douglas firs. It was the kind of place you expected Ewoks to emerge from. I rewarded myself with toasted Montreal-style garlic bagels from Siegel's or a pricey slice of veggie "Aphrodite" at the Flying Wedge, a pizza joint owned by three University of British Columbia art grads. I walked around the Seawall with briny sea in my nose, circling the fabled Stanley Park countless times. I walked seedy Granville Street with all its dumps and dives and landed a one-day job selling silver rings with skull heads and howling wolves on them. I didn't pan out as a vendor. My first sale was accidentally and grossly underpriced and whatever income I was supposed to make for the day was owed back to the guy who owned the stall.

I walked Davie Street, of course. This was the whole point of transplanting myself out west—to find the big missing chunk that

I couldn't pinpoint. It was just like the documentary I'd seen back in Brantford, complete with flapping rainbow flags, hookers and all the stereotypical buff guys with little dogs and baseball teams of lesbians drinking beer. Dax would later inform me that this was called "cruising," not walking.

I walked to (clothing optional) Wreck Beach with a copy of Tom Robbins's *Still Life with Woodpecker*. During the days that followed, I went back to the beach with *Jitterbug Perfume, Skinny Legs and All* and *Even Cowgirls Get the Blues*. Although I didn't opt out of all my clothes, I took it all in like a sponge. This was everything my sheltered self had imagined as gay utopia. There was a permanent skunky haze in the air, along with tequila shots, moose meat burgers and banana muffins.

One of the first letters my mom sent me in Vancouver was her assurance that she understood my need to get away. She had read a book about "emotional geography" and knew I was keen to explore mine. Of course, she would have preferred me carrying out this exploration closer to home, but it was better than me walking across Canada or joining that cult planting trees in California. Or baking ciabattas in Australia.

I was designing my own university experience, field trips and curricula. The program included these electives, in no particular order:

- Clayoquot Sound Civil Disobedience
- Dumpster Diving
- The Philosophy behind Clothing-Optional Beaches
- How to Make Stuff out of Found Feathers and Sand Dollars and Spend All Day Doing It
- The Literature of Robbins and Salinger
- The Deep Ecology of Vargas Island, BC (where a roomie

named Liz and I spent a week eating wet rice cakes and watching orcas, thanks to a guy named Gus who dropped us off for ten bucks and came back a week later to pick us up)

- *How to Live on Nothing*

Rick soon joined me in my roaming. He had dropped out of his program at Emily Carr, frustrated and overwhelmed by the demands, but he continued to paint in his own time. We built roaring fires with scraps of wood from nearby construction sites. When our wood source became scarce, we turned the oven on to broil and heated the kitchen that way. Was hydro included in the rent? Must have been. Fleetwood Mac was a constant. Rick smoked, he painted, I made stuff out of sand dollars (which has its limits, as you can imagine). He made his half-dozen hot dogs and we drank care-package powdered coffee further sweetened with our creative/semi-broke budget idea: melted cinnamon hearts in lieu of sugar.

Then one day, Daniel's penis was gone. When *Cockroach* fizzled, he moved back to Ottawa with Liz and Toumbi. An architect from Guelph (also named Rick) moved in for less than a month. Rick (my Rick, who I shared a room and shoebox cat with) invited his cousin Curtis to move in. And then Dan (the movie extra/perogy fiend) moved out, and Alex from Quebec moved in with "Replay." The dog's name was really Ripley, but with Alex's accent, we thought it was Replay. I'm probably missing a few roomies in the mix there. It was a true revolving door.

To boot, the little house was haunted, and the cats and dog were well aware of this. They would "watch"

Remember that classic Edward Packard *Choose Your Own Adventure* series? As the reader, you had all the power of the book's protagonist and determined the character's actions and outcome. Over and over. The books were marvellous—you could flip to any page of your choosing and end every story differently. At age eighteen, I had become that *Choose Your Own Adventure* main character. •

something move about the room, fur all hackled up. Replay would snarl while the cats would get their haunches up, as we did. I felt like a jittery horror film character trapped in one of those tingly scenes with a pounding heart in surround sound. The furniture in our house would start moving around spontaneously and almost always at night. Eventually, we became accustomed to this other-worldly disruption—but Shannon still wanted someone to "clean" our house. Not Molly Maid–style: our house needed to be cleansed with a smudging ceremony (Shannon was Cree, while Rick and Curtis were both Blackfoot), and all the mirrors in the house were covered. There was talk of someone being murdered upstairs in the 1940s. We were told to leave an offering outside the back door—fruit, bread, tobacco—whatever we deemed suitable.

It should come as no surprise that keeping tabs on ghosts and reading all of Tom Robbins's books didn't amount to any sort of income. So I did puppet shows at a local nature centre, but that didn't pay either. I thought about tree planting in northern BC, but who could I meet in the woods? I made another cinnamon-heart-sweetened coffee instead and pressed Play on Fleetwood Mac's "Everywhere." I was truly everywhere and all over the map again.

I applied to Canada World Youth for a nine-month exchange program to a developing country. I had met two guys who were in the program. Half of the exchange was spent doing meaningful volunteer work in Canada (I was really good at doing things for free) and the other half in a developing country such as Ecuador, digging pit toilets or wells. On the selection weekend, a hundred other candidates and I made a communal lunch of stir-fry with bok choy (which I'd never seen or heard of), demonstrating our co-operative skills and talking about issues that might arise in a developing country. There was a hot debate over how the queer candidates would react to an anti-gay parade in our host country. I was a little too rigid in my gayness and was willing to over-shadow the religion, beliefs and friendship of my host family in Ecuador, or wherever, for my cause and equality. I felt safe and gay in Canada, and I was teenybopper unaware of the tragic consequences that gender preference caused in other countries. There was no negotiating my loud and proud stance. And no, I wouldn't remove my nose ring or stop wearing my camouflage pants if either were deemed offensive to the host family. I wasn't that "Yes, man!" Canada World Youth was looking for. Other candidates proved they would be better at digging pit toilets in Cuenca or Guayaquil than me. So I walked out, my nose-ringed head held high, naively waving my invisible rainbow flag.

I tried to hold my head even higher when I returned home to visit my family nine months later. Especially when Ivan, my land-lord in Vancouver, called my parents to say that he was sorry, but he was evicting me and all my misfit roomies. Ivan was kind enough to send my worldly belongings back "home" in one single box: my Crayola pencil crayons, my sketchbook, some English Bay sand dollars and, accidentally, a pair of Rick's Nikes.

My Bohemian Rhapsody had come to an end—but with a Cherry on top.

8.

A House with No Walls

AFTER A FEW WEEKS back home, I decided to go to Costa Rica. It all made sense to follow up my dumpster-diving experiments with a jungle expedition. When you're not sure what to do with yourself, why not go to the jungle to sort it all out? I had no reason to return to Vancouver. With no place to live and scattered roommates (there was no email then, or Facebook or cellphones), it had lost its appeal. There was the no job thing too. Cherry ended up being my sole sexual conquest, an impressive addition to my Beginner Lesbian resumé. I was now a bona fide journalist and official queer.

Once I was back in Brantford, I'd found a tiny ad for participants to volunteer in a developing country. Maybe Guyana (where?), the Solomon Islands (where?) or Costa Rica (knew that one), where fluency in Spanish (nope) would be helpful. Youth Challenge International (YCI) was similar to the Canada World Youth program, but instead of having volunteers visit a developing country and then spend time in Canada, the project was based solely in the developing country. The $3,750 price tag for volunteering included round-trip airfare, building supplies for community projects, rice and beans (because that's all we'd be eating) and the opportunity of a lifetime. I smartly decided to not be such a hothead activist during my interviews. After an intense three-month Spanish course at the local college, I'd learned how to say "*El gato es negro.*" As long as I saw a black cat in Costa Rica, I was set. I also had to raise nearly four thousand dollars in less than six months. I'd never owned that much money in my life. I was twenty and more broke than when I had landed in Vancouver as a thousandaire. Kiley refused to buy my jean jacket one more time, so I was forced into all sorts of creative schemes. Utilizing my skills with wire hangers and my Nan's nylons, I made nylon saguaro cacti, spray-painted and stuffed with cotton balls, and planted them in painted pots (some leftover Hippoflowerpotamuses from the defunct Project Australia). These were a quick twenty-dollar item. I made dozens of Fimo polymer clay necklaces and sold them. I illustrated a twelve-month calendar of abstract lizards and sold it door to door. I visited a local screen printer and had a hundred T-shirts made to fund my mission: YCI Proyecto 6, Costa Rica 1994–95. The shirts were cheap and wide enough to fit two people in them, but each provided another quick twenty dollars. I did everything and sold anything to make Costa Rica happen.

I spent inordinate amounts of time in Toronto prior to my jungle stint. The YCI headquarters were conveniently located just north of Queen Street and a hundred paces from the Black Bull Tavern. I dutifully went to the YCI fundraising meetings as scheduled, and I also reconnected with a high school acquaintance who was attending university downtown. When I came back from Vancouver, the switchboards had lit up at my parents' home. I had made the "Guess who's gay?" list.

Laura, whom I knew from high school, introduced me to Tango, then the only lesbo bar on Church Street. It was a subterranean place with lots of sublevels and nooks for making out. A silver-haired fox named Maddy tended bar. Laura was living in her own apartment with a ginger-haired girlfriend, two hairless cats and an exceptionally large poster of Marlene Dietrich. I told Laura about Cherry, the Lotus, Wreck Beach and Chrystos (and how I was ready to re-enact some of that poetry on a woman). We moved on from grasshopper shots to play pool upstairs, packed to sweaty capacity. I was better at drinking beer than playing pool, so I kept pace and kept my back to the wall.

Dienne approached me, chalking the tip of her pool cue with a smirk. She had her own crew with her, and I could feel the eyes of all six of them on me as she leaned in. Admittedly I had been watching her, and she'd noticed. She asked me if I wanted to play, and I looked to Laura for backup. She shrugged and I agreed. The encounter moved at warp speed. I went home with Dienne that night, to her fancy downtown condo, and was quickly swept away by all her affection. I felt like Julia Roberts in *Pretty Woman* because she showered me with gifts. She bought me a North Face jacket on our second "date." She had lobster flown in from Nova Scotia (where she was from) and a bottle of Dom Pérignon on ice. It was all very fast-forward, and we progressed into a misguided relationship of sorts (I was twenty; she was thirty-five). I was outfitted with new jeans, Eddie Bauer plaid shirts (I'm not sure if that was ever a good look), Mary Chapin Carpenter CDs—anything and everything I ever mentioned in passing. She took me to fancy-pants restaurants where they served *boeuf bourguignon* and lamb vindaloo. She managed to nab front-row tickets to every big performer's concerts, including Mary Chapin.

Dienne was disappointed that I had to skip a weekend visit with her to have my wisdom teeth removed before my jungle sabbatical. She sent an over-the-top care package as I was convalescing. She knew that I liked Smarties, and she sent one hundred boxes by UPS. She also knew I was leaving for Costa Rica in a month and I was starting to get overwhelmed by all the attention and retail affection. She had a "father issue" and was paranoid to cross paths with my dad, so when she did come to Brantford, it was a hurried driveway pickup or drop-off. She wanted me in Toronto all the time.

Furthermore, my mind was already unfairly on a plane to San José. I certainly wasn't well versed in relationships, but I knew things were curdling. When my phone calls slowed, Dienne's true colours shone through, just like in the Cyndi Lauper song. There were extensive silent treatments when I did visit (she was better at them than my kid sister) and jealous rants. We stopped leaving her apartment (and we'd only been dating a month) because she was so fearful that I'd find someone else. She blew up on her best friend because she thought she was interested in me. She didn't like Laura being around either. She didn't want me to go to the jungle—instead, she let me know that it would be best if I moved in with her. (Years later, I would knowingly nod along to a sketch by comic Elvira Kurt: "Isn't it funny how we spend more time looking for the right pair of sunglasses than a girlfriend?" She was right. You could try on thirty pairs of sunglasses, but if some woman expressed interest in you? All in. I shoulder some blame for that.) And then Dienne disclosed that she had fallen for me because I looked exactly like her ex-girlfriend. Her ex-girlfriend who had died. Freaked out and fed up, I said we were done. I packed up the few things I had at her apartment and walked to the Greyhound bus station on Bay Street to buy a ticket back to Brantford.

One night at Tango, I told Laura about the living nightmare that Dienne had become. I headed downstairs to use the washroom before we had another beer. I sat down on the toilet to see a huge heart with my name and Dienne's initials scratched on the back of the door, with the date our relationship began and in even bigger font the day we broke up and "THE END!!!" I couldn't get to the Costa Rican jungle fast enough.

It was just before Christmas when our group landed in Central America. Starry-eyed, we assembled in a dorm-style building and had several meetings about cultural sensitivity, Spanish lessons and information sessions on project options. Our group of sixty volunteers from Canada and Australia would divide into five groups and five projects across Costa Rica. I wanted the most remote, jungly one, not the ones in city locales with primary health-care initiatives. To properly prepare, I asked Tia, a participant from Vancouver with a recently shaved head, to cut my hair off too. My below-the-shoulder blond locks were lopped off without a whole lot of finesse, as Tia had zero salon credentials—just a shaved head. Phil (the leader of our pack) said I looked like Ladyhawke, a reference I didn't get at the time, but I liked the handle.

The project I chose would start in the Monteverde rainforest, where we would help rebuild a *refugio* (a cabin to be used by guides in the park), map trails and identify local flora and fauna. If you are willing to volunteer, you get to do crazy things that you have no experience with. Most of us had never bothered with a hammer before and had only coloured maps in geography class. What they failed to mention was that it rains every single day in the *rain*forest. Our tribe of twelve would then move on into an even deeper, denser outpost in Alto Cuen. Here we would build a structure for visiting North American doctors who would provide health care and resources to the local villagers. It seemed like a great do-gooder goal, but why in the world would anyone send a bunch of awkward, unskilled teens into a jungle to build something of this magnitude? We were assisting local labourers, of course, but this was Habitat for Humanity taken to the next, next level. We had no safety boots or hard hats or expertise or experts who spoke English.

The experience was truly seismic—as we ended up sleeping in the vibration zone of the very active Arenal Volcano. It rumbled every half-hour. At night you could see trickles of molten neon lava worming its way down from the mouth of the volcano. I went from sleeping with a gay man and a cat in a shoebox to sleeping with a woman who loved me because I looked like her dead girlfriend to sleeping in a jungle hut with no walls in the lava path of a volcano.

Our motley crew was responsible for maintaining a daylong fire, as it was our only cooking source. We rotated every few days, sharing responsibilities like cooking rice (over an open fire! I'd never even made rice successfully at home) and adding iodine to the river water so we could safely drink it. Yes, the same river water that we bathed in with the swimming village pigs. Our group was a twelve-kilometre rubber-boot hike (with six river crossings) to the nearest shack that sold flour, some tiny chocolate bars, nails, gas and *yuca* (cassava). We lost radio contact almost immediately, despite our extensive lessons on operating a two-way radio with headquarters.

The Indigenous Cabécar villagers looked at us blankly. The bravest of the bunch (the kids) scurried around and made attempts at touching our blond hair and peeling sunburned skin from our shoulders. We were pretty much like aliens. Some of the local women were topless, and the shaman wore wild-pig teeth around his neck. His hut had a jaguar skin hanging in the rafters. I'd seen stuff like this before in *National Geographic*, so the culture shock wasn't that overwhelming.

Most of us had never done anything that was now expected of us before. None of us had prepared meals for a dozen people with only rice, canned mackerel, bananas and gnarly *yuca* root as ingredients. We came as prepared as we could be for this experience, our packs stuffed with all that we thought was essential for three months in the jungle (two pairs of pants, two T-shirts, two long-sleeved shirts, two of everything). But in two weeks' time in that rainy rainforest, everything went sour. Nothing dried in the humid clime. Cameras (film-style) stopped working and journals grew in size, not from words but from humidity swelling the paper. Our sleeping bags were super punky, both from piggy river baths and jungle sweat.

And there were twelve of us in a house with no walls. Four from Australia, six from Canada and two from Costa Rica. For the initial project in Monteverde, one of the Aussie gals and I became self-proclaimed chief cartographers and illustrators for the trail maps, while the rest of our group wielded machetes to create the trails. Our crew had the still-standing old *refugio* to bunk in while the new one was being constructed. We had oranges and toucans at our doorstep at both locations.

When we moved to Alto Cuen for the second phase of our project, a grand hut was kindly "leased" to us by the village chief. A group of pigs slept below us, and cockroaches as big as Pop-Tarts skittered about in the palm-frond roof above us. The floor was a patchwork of limbs covered in sheets of bark (and our sleeping bags and worldly gear), with a tangle of mosquito nets tied to the main timber frame like a spiderweb. Our kitchen? Totally open-air. *En plein air*, as the French would say. I don't know what the Spanish would say—definitely not *el gato es negro*. There was a small firepit and a crude pantry that had to be out of reach of the pigs and free-range chickens. Our fancy ensuite was a pit toilet. You had to hang on to a stick for dear life with one hand (so you didn't fall in) while trying to create a bowel movement after a steady feed of rice, black beans, bananas and peanut butter. We had oatmeal for breakfast, just to add to the beige diet. Bowel movements weren't an issue for very long, though. They became so frequent that constipation was something we all craved.

After a while, a few of us complained about our limbs falling asleep—and staying asleep. In the morning, whether it was from sleeping on a tree-bark floor, malnutrition from the beige diet or a side effect of the anti-malaria drug chloroquine, it took a good hour to get the tingles out. On top of that, we were covered in mystery bites. Rachel, a Canadian counterpart from Charlottetown, PEI, developed some form of a flesh-eating disease on her legs. I had a botfly larva growing in my calf, while poor Tomas, the only Aussie lad, had about six in his head.

It was gruesome all around. Jungle fun consisted of gathering around Tomas's head after it was shaved and covered in duct tape for the day of the Great Worm Reveal. Two local boys that hung around our group had been picking around Tomas's head when he visibly started scratching. My bite appeared like a marble under the surface of my skin, and flies wouldn't stop congregating around the wound. Tomas and I later learned that this was the breathing hole for the larva. The kids started getting hyper, jumping up and down and shouting, "*Lingwa! Lingwa!*" We quickly learned this meant "worm!"

Jungle surgery was this: covering the bites with big gobs of Vaseline to suffocate the larva and plug up its breathing hole. For the next five hours, both of us (Tomas to a larger degree) went through the very painful throes of the larvae suffocating. The worm actually moved around a lot and would stop me dead in my tracks with electric, hot-poker pain. The only way to remove them is by squeezing them out. Tomas went first, and as our leader squished out the projectile larvae one by one from Tomas's scalp, we all freaked out. Tomas had the distinct treat of squeezing my left calf to eject my pet worm. It was all just about unbearable. And those were the worms we could see. Three months later, I would return home with three kinds of parasites in my gut and another in my foot. Tapeworms, roundworms—the whole jungle all-inclusive package.

More unsettling was the trench foot that set in. Our boots were never dry from all the river crossings and rain. When our feet didn't itch like our socks were full of poison ivy, they just fell apart. The only remedy was a magic powder that I was able to obtain when Alex chopped off half his thumb with a machete, necessitating a walk into the nearest village for stitches and meds—and access to ice cream, Coca-Cola and our mail from afar. And trench-foot powder.

Scorpions made homes in our wellies (rain boots) overnight, and each morning began with a swift emptying of the boots before any trench foot was put inside. We all accumulated scars, fourteen-day runs of diarrhea, malaria, strange rashes and severe gut rot.

Before we had left Toronto, our leader, Phil, had suggested we eat as many doughnuts as we could. "You'll be dreaming of these, I promise." I took one and shrugged off the advice. He was so right. The lacklustre menu had me fantasizing in a chronic state of hunger and diarrhea. All I talked about in my diary was the stuff I couldn't wait to eat again: deep-fried pineapple chicken balls in that sweet Day-Glo yellow sauce, Kentucky Fried Chicken, all-dressed chips, Crunchie bars, chocolate milk, greasy fries from George's chip stand saturated with vinegar and salt. A Burger King Whopper. Mom's roast beef with a glass of gravy. Her peanut butter chocolate chip cookies. Those stupid Hawaiian sprinkle doughnuts.

And socks. I wanted dry socks more than Whoppers and Big Macs.

Any sweets sent from home were rationed like money stuffed under a mattress. I was so selfish I almost got lost in the jungle, forever, because of it. One day I was in the day hut, napping and letter writing, as was the perk of kitchen duty. After feeding the gang, doing dishes at the river, boiling more drinking water, stoking the fire and prepping for the next canned mackerel and rice feed, you earned downtime. It was late, late afternoon, and in the Alto Cuen valley, sundown was sudden. I noticed the change in light in the palm frond shadows but carried on. I had one last chocolate bar that I didn't want to share. I ate it in tiny mouse bites, savouring every stale bit of it. The light on my headlamp was dying as fast as the day's sun. I finished the chocolate bar, going so far as to lick the wrapper (as one does in private) and then licked the stamp on my letter home.

I set off on the path back to the other hut, where Tomas had probably thoughtfully started the rice (he was my kitchen duty partner and worm confidant). The walk should have taken only seven minutes. I'd surpassed that and felt ferns whipping at my thighs—too high for the path. I turned back a bit and followed the right path, scolding myself for veering off so easily. I walked into waist-high thorns and vines that curled up into the canopy. I turned to the right. And left. I started a nervous jog but didn't get far with the roots that tripped up my feet. I was so far off the path that I was in a thicket of dark vegetation. It was primo hour for malaria and I was totally exposed. I started to yell. I called out every single person's name in our group. No answer. I yelled until I was hoarse and shaking and stumbling about like a crazed person. It was pitch-black already, and my headlamp was no brighter than a tea light in the wind. I turned it off to save the batteries in case I was in it for the long haul.

All sorts of sordid scenarios entered my mind. Jaguars. Malaria. Drug runners (we saw them daily, passing by our camp with flour sacks full of marijuana, AK-47s casually slung over their shoulders). Did I want to yell and attract drug runners? Talk about a great crime of opportunity. My biggest childhood fear of being kidnapped was about to come to fruition. I was going to be in the *Brantford Expositor*—not as a guest columnist but as a kidnap story from the jungles of Alto Cuen. All because of pure selfishness and a rather crappy chocolate bar. Poor, selfish Ladyhawke.

I sobbed a bit and swatted away mosquitoes and moths as big as my head. I yelled and yelled until I heard a sound. I yelled whatever I last hollered and heard the human sound again. It wasn't a word, more of a "boop" that was getting louder. Yell, boop, yell, boop. I was frantic. At this point, I was okay with drug runners finding me because it had to be better than spending the night and maybe my life in the jungle alone.

I turned on my waning light and saw a barefoot, bare-chested man shorter than me approach. A woman followed, shirtless, with a baby. They were Cabécar. Imagine their surprise in finding me. Blond hair! Blue eyes! My new friends immediately turned and left. I stopped them short and pulled out a pad of paper and marker to play Pictionary. I drew a cross to represent the church in the village. I drew a helicopter pad and helicopter (not knowing if they'd actually seen a helicopter before). I drew the soccer field in the village and a picture of the hut I was living in, which looked like every other hut in the jungle. The man cleared his throat and kept walking. Unsure if I was to follow or not, I did anyway.

It seemed like eternity, as these moments do, when life flashes all sorts of irrational things through your brain. Then the family stopped abruptly in front of me and the man pointed to a distant glow. I craned my neck to see kerosene lamps hanging from a hut and a small fire. We were the only ones in the village with kerosene lamps. It was my hut! My home! My home with no walls! I gave the poor villager an unexpected hug. I wanted to cry and throw up all at once. The young family turned and disappeared as quickly as they had appeared in the black of the jungle.

I ran, half sobbing, toward the hut. Tomas had started the rice. Alice had her nose in her Spanish dictionary. Alex was playing his faux drums, and Tia and Kirsty were playing something like euchre in the corner. Shaye was picking at her guitar, singing Eric Clapton's "Tears in Heaven." (And her tears *are* in heaven now. Shaye Martirano was hit and killed by a car in 2002.) No one had missed me. They figured I was at the other hut, writing letters—which I was. Until I was totally lost. I made them all listen to my drama-in-real-life moment and all was laughed about in the end. (But I left out the part about the hoarded chocolate bar.)

By this point, two months into communal living, we were starting to get itchy (not just because of the trench foot). Even though Mark Burnett hadn't produced *Survivor* yet, I still wanted to vote a few people out of the jungle. I'm not so cheeky to think that I wouldn't have landed a few votes, too. The rain never stopped. Our spines were universally compressed from hauling packs filled with river boulders for the latrine. We hauled in boxes of nails, chainsaws, ten-foot sheets of corrugated steel, bags of hammers, shovels—all while wearing rubber boots. We hauled canisters of kerosene and five-pound buckets of peanut butter, fifty-pound sacks of rice, cement and papayas. Our enthusiasm was at an all-time low for digging the latrine and piecing together a clinic outpost for doctors that might possibly arrive in the future. On one of our walks back to the nearest town, Phil pointed out a similar building that UNICEF had built. It was long empty and appeared to have not been used. Ever.

I wondered about our collective selfless act of volunteering in this "developing" country. Were my motives genuinely locked in sustainable community projects, or was I keener on developing myself somewhere exotic versus in my Brantford bedroom? I was guilty of buying an experience—all of us were. The notion that our privilege and entitlement had financed this life-shaping opportunity in a "poor" country wouldn't sink in for most of us for a few more years. I was reading Paulo Coelho (*The Alchemist*) and *Siddhartha* and other Buddhist writings. I was full of existential theories and trying to see things on the flip side. I was also full of parasites.

Near the end of our project (amazingly, after the roof tresses were successfully raised, it looked like a genuine, solid structure), the rains became so severe that the only suspension bridge washed away. My parents were reading reports at home of the massive floods in the Dole banana plantations (exactly where we were— we witnessed the sinewy men swinging unripe banana bunches across the river on cables). The river was so angry with volume that you could hear rocks rolling along its bottom at night. The water (our drinking water) was the colour of chocolate milk. And we had no radio contact. The plan was to hike out and meet the rest of the extended YCI group back in San José a few days later. We hadn't seen the big group since we parted ways before Christmas. Some inter-group letters were circulated once, but largely, our group of twelve had been solitary and remote, as advertised.

We all had varying degrees of stomach cramps and chronic diarrhea. Cheri, Shaye and I were laid up with what was definitely the potent punch of malaria. The chills were like being stuck in a chest freezer for days. Then we had the sweats, saturating our sleeping bags like we'd been hosed down. The malaria headache is a game changer. Imagine having an axe stuck in your head. We were so weak that walking out of the jungle was impossible. I couldn't even make it to the pit toilet and had shit my pants a few times already, unable to pull on my rubber boots fast enough. I didn't even care about scorpions being in my boot bottoms at that point.

We couldn't hike out if we wanted to. The river was running too high and fast. We'd already almost lost Alice to a mishap when the horses we were using to run gear over the river spooked. Alice was dragged under when the rope snagged her pack and the horses kicked up and ran downstream. It was hard to believe that the very scenarios we had "play-acted" back in Mono Mills, Ontario, on a YCI selection weekend would actually happen. The pigs got into our food supply again. Shaye had to be extracted from our first location in Monteverde on a C-spine board when severe asthma and our altitude in the cloud forest made breathing impossible for her.

When a helicopter landed in Alto Cuen to deliver emergency food supplies to the village, the G.I. Joe–looking army crew happened upon us, a group of white people stranded in the jungle. Phil spoke with the pilot and said we had to be in San José in two days. We were trapped because of the floods and unable to contact our headquarters. The pilot promised he would circle back at the end of the day and evacuate us. We hurriedly packed our gear, weak and beaten from the elements, but electrified with thoughts of a helicopter rescue. The villagers didn't have the luxury of simply lifting off and relocating like we did; the flooded banana plantations impacted the livelihood of so many, but I was too young to comprehend all of this. I was greedily focused on getting back to my cozy life and pineapple chicken balls. I'd had enough of personal development.

The helicopter didn't return. We waited by the helicopter pad until dark. We lit lamps and strained to hear that welcome hum of a chopper that didn't appear. We waited the next day too. There was no time to start a fire for breakfast—we had to hike down to the pad again and wait. The river still roared with the rainfall, and the villagers watched us from their huts and hammocks, waiting.

The helicopter that did come, much later that day, was a double-blade Chinook. It was so G.I. Joe that I couldn't believe this was my life! The camo crew landed and shuffled us into the back of the Chinook in jump seats that faced each other. It was massive inside and loud as hell. We were up and gone and out of our jungle existence so fast that I couldn't take it all in as much as I wanted. The palm fronds flattened and bent with the lift of the Chinook. The village kids ran out and waved madly back at us as we disappeared over their huts into our bigger reality.

The pilot hugged the swollen river for a bit and then drew up and over the jungle canopy to the east coast. The back of the Chinook was open, and despite our previous bitchy days with each other, we looked at each other with mad grins on our faces. Was this happening? We were flying low enough that we could see monkeys in the treetops and flocks of parrots taking flight.

We had left the jungle, but it wouldn't leave us. The enormity of the event wouldn't sink in until much, much later. In fact, ridding myself of parasites required a trip to the Infectious Diseases Clinic at McMaster University in Hamilton.

But I was home again.

Hello, dry socks and sprinkle doughnuts.

9.

Post-Jungle Blues

WHEN I RETURNED from the jungle, all Buddhist and enlightened by the self-imposed hardships that I had endured, I chose a bad adventure. I didn't know it at the time, of course.

I obviously "came out" in Vancouver, but I wasn't really out and about to all in Ontario, especially in my hometown. During my jungle furlough, my focus was on perfecting rice over the open fire and surviving trench foot. Anything gay was shelved in the face of the bigger picture, which was surviving the jungle. Coming out, in either province, wasn't as monumental as I thought it would be. I don't know if anyone was really surprised—I did wear that pantsuit to the prom, after all.

I had been gay inside my head for enough years that it was no longer a grand reveal. Telling my parents was more of a formality. I had jumped on the Greyhound bus to Toronto to attend the Pride parade with Laura. We even marched *in* the parade with all the swinging bare boobs (not ours) and glittery-chested guys.

Two boozy, wide-eyed days of enlightenment later, I was back at home, recounting the weekend to my mom in the kitchen. She was all ears and so was my dad, eavesdropping from the living room. He piped up, "What do you mean you were in the parade? Why were you in the parade?" And, cool as a cucumber, I said, "Because I'm gay." And he said, "Gay as in happy, right?" And then my mom said, "Larry!" And that was kind of the end of it. After being in the parade and meeting Sandy in a beer garden because I was also gay as in happy, I started coming home on the back of her motorcycle and that was that. Not only was I gay, but I also suddenly had a girlfriend with a Honda 450 and Rod Stewart hair. Which, at that time, was encouraged and du jour.

Sandy wasn't a bad adventure. She played ball hockey (despite recently breaking both legs skydiving), had faux adhesive stars on her ceiling and made a really nice chili. But during the brief Sandy chapter, there was also an unplanned crossover with a phys. ed. teacher, and that's where my heart became mouldy. Let's pretend I spilled an entire can of sticky root beer here, in this book, and a gallon of black oil paint over seven years of my life. If you try prying the pages open, they'll just tear and come off in a big chunk. I'm eager to fast-forward through these seven years, but here's a little plot summary. Let's rename the pivotal character to protect the innocent (me). "Sue Sylvester" and I had an affair. I had been with Sandy and her motorcycle for only a month or so. Sue had been in a relationship for more than eleven years, and when her partner learned of "us," she immediately severed ties, served Sue with a fifty-five-thousand-dollar settlement fee and moved out. Sue was twenty-two years older than me, which I now understand is unacceptable. At the time, I jumped on her bandwagon and her assurance that an age difference didn't matter. Upon reflection: yeah, maybe if you are 80 and 102, not 20 and 42.

But after Sandy rode her motorcycle off into the sunset, and Sue's girlfriend drove off into it shortly after in a truck, I moved in with Sue. She owned a house on the Grand River in a tiny town of five thousand in Dunnville, Ontario.

Sue said I needed to get a career, pronto. Carrying the mortgage and payout to her ex was not the stuff a secondary teacher's paycheque was cut out for. But Dunnville offered little in the area of career options. I was happy to pick strawberries at the local patch down the road, and they were advertising for seasonal pickers, but Sue said no. I needed an education and prestige, according to her. I have never been driven by money, which was not an attractive quality in Sue's mind.

I wanted to stay true to my calling and take another stab at writing full-time. Sue relented, and I enrolled in a Writing for Children correspondence course from the Ottawa Writing School. This was during the era when you actually snail-mailed stuff to the instructor. The course came with a series of cassette tape lessons to listen to each week as part of the coursework. After my first assignment (creating a personal profile), my instructor asked if I had ever considered exploiting my sexuality. In my profile, I mentioned that I was a lesbian (probably in capital letters, as I was a real flag-bearer at every given opportunity since gaining ground and comfort in my identity). When I said I was game for exploiting, I started to write erotica for money. (Not erotica for children, I should clarify: this was after I'd completed the Writing for Children course.) The first erotic short story I wrote earned me two hundred dollars (more than half of what I made in an entire month at *Cockroach*). I was in the big leagues now, and my story was included in Maxim Jakubowski's 1994 anthology *The Mammoth Book of Erotica*. The local paper caught wind of this and I was asked to pose on a cannon by the bridge (straddling it even, as per the photographer's request), and the reporter interviewed me about all the dirty details. There was also a follow-up *Globe and Mail* article about my experience as a student of erotica at the Ottawa Writing School. Not only was I writing, but people were writing about me! It was all very unexpected but definitely the launch of my semi-serious writing trajectory.

A year later, after patchy payments for my published work in erotica anthologies, Sue announced that my writing "lifestyle" was more hobby than career. While I still would have preferred strawberry picking, in June of 1997, I found myself writing an entrance exam to attend a private massage therapy college in Hamilton. Even though I didn't have a high school diploma, I could apply as a "mature student." While Sue can credit herself for pressuring me to get a career, it was Sharon from Bark Lake camp who inspired my choice of career back in 1991. I had signed up for Sharon's workshop on shiatsu techniques, and that night, Sharon said one sentence that became part of my matrix: "Massage is the greatest gift you can give someone." I really don't know what career I would have pulled out of my hat if I hadn't attended her workshop. I wanted to connect with people on a different level, and I'd found an unusual opportunity by writing erotica. Becoming a massage therapist allowed me to communicate in an unexpected way too. Not to sound mystical, but it became an outlet for diffusing my self-isolation and a way to connect. It was a puzzle piece that fit, despite my hesitation and doubts.

After an intense two-year program spent memorizing all 650 skeletal muscles and 206 bones in the human body, I became the career woman Sue wanted. In 1999, I passed the official (gruelling) Ontario College of Massage Therapists board exam to become a genuine Registered Massage Therapist. Most everyone was surprised that I had attained such credentials and an actual, practical, normal job instead of my usual makeshift income earned by cleaning turtle tanks, dipping candles and tie-dyeing crap all day. I had a true lucky break when the only massage therapist in Dunnville broke her wrist the very day that I received my successful exam results in the mail. I took over her business and clientele a few days later and opened my own clinic six months after that. I cheekily called my space the Upper Hand. If I didn't have it at home, I would have it at work!

Sue and I were often mistaken for mother and daughter. If we were in Hamilton, near the school where she taught, she told me to walk well ahead of her in case we ran into one of her students or another teacher. Our age difference was obviously glaring, but it wasn't an issue unless we were in public. I didn't grasp the enormity of this (as my family politely kept mum about it all) until our first Pride weekend together. Sue and I went to Slack Alice, the only total girl bar in Toronto. A tall, sophisticated femme woman wormed her way through the crowd to talk to me. She introduced herself with a confident handshake as Fran and said, "My friend Andie thinks you're cute." Fran pointed out Andie, who was blushing in the corner. We exchanged small waves. Fran ushered her over so we could properly meet (Sue was busy chugging beer and unaware). I told Andie that I was with Sue and pointed to her. Andie's reflex response was, "What are you doing with an old lady?" Andie was a year older than me, with caramel-blond hair and penetrating blue eyes. She was beautiful, sweet and attentive—the kind of person I should have been with. And she was dead right. What was I doing with the old lady?

I soon realized there was more wrong with our relationship than just our age difference. My "starter relationship" had long expired; there was so much focus on my personal development and career achievement that our relationship just went through the motions. We'd been living as oblivious roommates for years. We should have been friends, not lovers. There was no electricity between us. In the words of my mother, my relationship with Sue was truly fuckshit.

While establishing a career should have been the biggest event in my twenty-something life, next to snuffing out the toxic relationship with Sue, both events were overshadowed by my parents selling their house, *our* house, at RR#2.

It was Thanksgiving and all family members were accounted for—the "Original Five," as my dad would say. We had the traditional big bird stuffed and slathered in butter and sage in the oven. Potatoes were diced and bubbling over on the stovetop, ready to be drained and mashed. Dax probably had Madonna cranked, and my mom probably told him to "turn that Blondie off."

We were gathered in the living room around our wheat-sheath table when my mom slipped out into the kitchen and came back with a tray of champagne glasses. This was monumental. We never had champagne as a family or celebrated in such a fancy fashion. What the hell? Kiley, Dax and I were all equally startled. My mind began racing all sorts of places. My mom seemed happy about this toast, but my dad was sullen in his armchair, blankly eating a bowl of salted peanuts. And then my mom started to cry.

Oh God. Somebody was dying. Or were they getting divorced? Dax reached for a glass and we all followed suit. We might need to be intoxicated and heavily medicated after hearing whatever news my mom was about to deliver.

"What?" Dax asked.

Kiley's face was the colour of a powdered doughnut.

My mom gathered herself, raised a glass and blurted: "We bought a house!"

We clanked glasses so hard I thought they'd shatter. Flo was not thrilled. He loved our little brick ranch at RR#2. Even though he was a city boy through and through, my dad still loves that house so much that if my folks won the lottery, he would buy it back in a heartbeat. This is where it gets sentimental. The reason my dad didn't want to leave RR#2 was because of our dearly beloved but dearly departed pets, Moker, Whisper, Phantom, Drakkar and Xanadu. While the four cats were buried at the edge of our property in a flower bed by the train tracks, Xanadu had disappeared while I was living in Vancouver and was never found. Flo looked for him tirelessly, every night after work, calling for him while walking the fields and property lines, hoping Xanadu would come bounding up to him from the tall grasses. They say dogs will wander before they die. He was so old (we never knew his age when he was dropped off) that all the fur had fallen off his back and tail. He looked like an ancient anteater. He had teeth missing and cataracts that made his eyes milky blue. Our little Xanadu had lived a large life and was polite right until the end. He always went to the neighbouring field to relieve himself. Not once did he ever go on our two-acre property. Not finding him was nearly unbearable though, for all of us. He was such a loyal pup, always on our heels and at the end of my bed, like a stoic sentry. Dad was not so jazzed about the move because he'd be leaving Xanadu. This is what animals do to you. They become part of your very matrix. They are synonymous with home. How the hell do you leave them behind when their life's goal was to stay by your side?

I understood my mom's need to uproot, too. She had lived fifty years on the same road. She was tired of everything being so familiar and everyone knowing each other's movements. Country life is kind of like Big Brother in a drone with a Twitter account. People know what's happening in your life before you do and tweet about it in the produce aisle while squeezing melons.

Kiley, Dax and I had no idea my parents were looking to move. They didn't want to alarm us (more than a tray of champagne and sudden tears did) and were worried that we would be upset too. Yes, it was our childhood home, but my parents were certainly entitled to do whatever made their hearts pound, since we were all out of the house and following our own pounding hearts. Kiley had moved out to Banff immediately after finishing university, and Dax had moved to Toronto. And I moved to a town that celebrated catfish. We had successfully launched, and my parents were ready to do the same.

Yes, I would miss our childhood home and the spring peeper soundtrack. I'd miss the tall pines that I climbed to the tip-top of. I'd miss the swans gathering in the flooded fields in the spring. The kestrel on the power line. My arrowhead collection that I buried somewhere and never found again. The constant perfume of my grandfather's pig farm. The smell of tobacco curing in the kilns. The passing of the train on the tracks. The hum of small planes that flew low over our house from the nearby airport—so low that the pilots waved to us. I already missed Xanadu and our great little crew of pets. But the home, without them or my parents in it, quickly became a house. Home would be wherever they were, and we could take our stories with us. Kiley, Dax and I were given a photo album of RR#2, a total time capsule of our years as the Original Five.

To this day, my dad won't drive past our old house. I've been past a few times, eager to note the changes, which I don't mind seeing. The memory of that house is inside of me. The new owners of Grandma's house invited me in once. The black and white checkered linoleum was gone, as were the old glittery melamine countertops and the wringer washer that my grandmother threatened to run us through when we were hyper. It was completely updated, but I could still "see" the stories: "brushing" Sam with the corn broom around the kitchen, the party-line phone, hanging over the freezer chest to grab a TV dinner, the cabinet with a hundred salt and pepper shakers. I could almost smell Zest.

"She still visits us sometimes," the current owner, Judy, told me.

"Really?"

"We can hear her cough."

This I believed. No doubt Grandma was missing her weekly *National Enquirer* and smut papers for gossip. She had to eavesdrop on Judy from the other side—her cough was giving her away, just like it did on the party line. I looked around for a wayward puffball. Grandma sure loved them fried up with butter. Isn't it crazy how you can smell those memories?

Years later, in Uganda, I would meet a local named Richard. He walked alongside me in the botanical gardens that were full of the fragrant nightshade-family flower called yesterday-today-and-tomorrow (also known as the morning-noon-and-night or kiss-me-quick plant). The flowers last for three days and change colour with each day. The first day they are purple (yesterday), the second day they change to a pastel lavender shade (today), and on the third day they change to an almost white colour (tomorrow). I couldn't get enough of their sweet smell. Richard said, "Can you hear the smell?" I don't know if it was a lost-in-translation moment, but, you know, I *could* hear it. I can still hear the smell of the tobacco kiln and pig manure, too.

The move to the city was enormous for my parents, and Mom visibly bloomed with her changed surroundings. My dad came around eventually. After fifty years on the same road, life began anew, as it can. Maybe the restlessness that spurred my parents' move was contagious. I wanted to uproot and hit reset just as they did. I wanted to box up my life and unfold it somewhere else. I wasn't actively looking for love, that's for sure.

But I found it on a boat, of all places, during Pride weekend in Toronto. It slapped me right across my suntanned face. I fell in love—the kind that heart-rending poems are written about and cowboys shoot allies over. At the stale, tail end of my relationship with Sue, friends had convinced us to buy tickets for a women's boat cruise around Toronto Islands—it quickly felt like a reunion, with so many familiar faces. When I saw her, everything in my periphery blurred. I could see only her. She had stitches train-tracked across her nose and forehead from a recent dragon-boating incident, but I could see nothing but gorgeous. She was the one; I knew in an instant. I wanted to sail off into the syrupy sunset with her right then, but she looked rather happy with the buff woman whose hand was interlocked in hers. She pushed her sunglasses up onto the top of her head, and when I looked into her eyes for the first time I was a goner, but our sunset sail would have to wait a few years.

As Sue and I moved around the boat that day, I made excuses to drift back to this woman, whose name, I learned, was Kim. I could sense her presence and my heart rate responded. She wore a grey "ARMY" T-shirt, baggy white cargos and Timberland boots. I smiled to see that her girlfriend was similarly dressed, wearing a "NAVY" tee, but the same boots. I always laughed at couples that started dressing alike—but when I met Kim, I wanted to be her T-shirt twin. I lingered, hanging on to her stories and smiling at her bent-over laugh. I wanted to be the one to make her laugh like that, all of the time.

I loved Kim in that superhuman way that allows you to flip cars and move boulders to rescue trapped people. Her smiley eyes warmed my mildewed heart, and I buzzed like I was on a caffeine high the entire time she was within reach. I mean, she looked hot even with twenty stitches stamped across her face. Most people would turn away at the sight of such a banged-up face still bruised and raw. I couldn't look away. While everyone else on that boat cruise was wilting in the sun, sweaty and drippy and sour from the heat, Kim was neatly pressed and smelled like coconuts and Lanvin. Every hair was where it should be, her lips were glossed, her clothes immaculate. Her skin was a beautiful bronze, like honey and milk chocolate. I couldn't get enough of her. Her teeth—they were Hollywood white, and the peppermint gum she casually chewed instantly locked into my olfactory sense. Every day that followed, if I smelled peppermint, I thought of Kim. Any residual feelings I had for Sue evaporated.

Nearly a year later, we inevitably fell into each other's arms. After a night at a bar, a group of us grabbed a taxi back to a friend's house where we were sleeping over. Kim and I didn't sleep—instead we talked until dawn, which became our routine. As the sun rose, the distance between us became closer. We spoke in whispers, well aware of our partners sleeping in nearby rooms. We kissed, that peppermint gum flavour was on my tongue, and there was no going back. We swapped stories about our current

Thoughts on Sour-Milk Relationships
Pretend you're going on a vacation for a week. You have a little milk left in the carton, and maybe it will still be good when you come back. The expiry date is always overly encouraging. But when you come back ten days later, you know it's going to be off. What is it with that temptation thing—that human need to open it and see just how awful it is? How bad does it smell? Better yet, if you have someone to share the awful with: "Here, you gotta smell this."

I'm not opening that carton again; I'm throwing it out and taking it to the curb. (Just so you know, I'd feel too guilty about being environmentally unfriendly to actually do this. I'd dump the clotted milk down the drain, rinse the sour container and then properly recycle it.) Maybe that's what sour-milk relationships are all about: learning how to recycle used-up emotions and ideals, then reclaim and repurpose them. •

girlfriends and the running list of reasons why we both needed to move on. We were desperate for something so simple—kindness. Kim had such gentle ways. She would give the Boy Scouts at the grocery store a ten-dollar donation for one apple. She was generous not just with money but with her time and love.

As things ramped up, Kim split from her girlfriend, but she still had a shared house to sell and furniture to divide. I left Sue and found a cheap bedroom for rent in Burlington. I was happy to finally be closer to Kim, regardless of the minefield that seemed to surround us. Kim was emotionally consistent, and her smiley eyes made everything in the world right again. I took a deep dive into her heart without looking back. Kim said thank you. For everything. I felt so much relief being away from Sue. But both of us were still dealing with the fallout of our breakups and the messy aftermath of stuff, friends and money. We were exhausted from our exes and the fury that was still going on.

For Kim and me, as strong as our connection was, our timing wasn't right. After a starry-eyed year together, we parted—but it was never about lost love. That was the crazy thing; we still loved each other. There was no anger, no bitterness, no yelling. I'm not sure who cried more. I was a blubbering mess. I cried my head off looking at our photos from Holguin and Amsterdam. I cried until I felt sick and cried more until I yawned and ran dry. I retraced my two tattoos, indelibly (and happily) linked to Kim. Like a true sad sack, I kept her broken hockey stick blade that I was supposed to throw out when she replaced it after a game. I kept a pair of her wool socks that were forgotten in my laundry basket. I stopped sleeping and felt like I was walking on bones with no cartilage left. I couldn't stop loving her. I tortured myself by drifting through the Eaton's Centre to spray her Lanvin cologne on my wrist. Can you hear the smell? I could. Although I didn't want to believe it at the time, Kim was right: the two of us were totally frayed from our exes and needed to regroup. I trusted her heart and somehow knew that it wouldn't be our end, not for good. When we ended, we somehow began all at once.

I was on the brink of something. A meltdown or breakdown or shakedown.

Without Kim, there was no point in staying in Burlington. I'd been commuting to my job as a massage therapist at the Fairmont Royal York Hotel in downtown Toronto. It made sense to be near there instead. My GPS settings were recalibrated to the Village and a one-bedroom apartment in a brownstone on the corner of Church and Gloucester. This was where the gays were, and I thought I might as well join them.

I was free to a good home again.

10.

Existential Crisis: Toronto

"YOUR SOUND SYSTEM is both impressive and invasive. Please remember that you're not the only one who lives here. APT. 20!" This was the welcome-wagon message taped to my apartment door in the Village on day two.

Sarah McLachlan's *Afterglow* was one of my faves at this time. Jann Arden's "Could I Be Your Girl?" and "Thing for You" were also on my breakup soundtrack. Plus "The First Cut Is the Deepest" (Sheryl Crow's take) and Lara Fabian's "I Will Love Again." Over and over. Kim and Kim and Kim. If "saptacular" were a word, that would have described me. I was heart-shattered but trying to be buoyed by my change of address and shiny new independence. It was the first time I had ever lived alone, without a mélange of roomies at every turn. Toronto was such a bigger, taller version of Vancouver, and I had some street sense to learn, quick.

On day three, I was ripped off by the charismatic guy who lived next door to me, in apartment 14, who needed twenty bucks for gas. He seemed genuine and held a jerry can in his left hand. "I live right beside you—hell, I'll give you my leather jacket as collateral until I get back if you'd like." I thought, *What would Kim do?* She'd give the guy twenty bucks in a heartbeat. I trusted him in the way that jerry-can-scam guys like him rely on for their livelihood. I offered him an extra ten bucks, as Kim would have, just to be sure he'd be okay. I didn't need his leather jacket for collateral. "I trust you. No problem! I know where you live!" His car was clearly out of gas (he had pointed to it, parked outside the building). "I'm going to run over to the gas station on Wellesley and Sherbourne and fill this jerry can and get to the ATM. I'll pay you back straight after." Right. A few days passed. No one lived in that apartment. I knocked every time I went past. For two weeks. Until someone actually moved in three months later.

My two-storey brownstone was in the beating heart of the Village. It was the most logical place to move as a Toronto greenhorn, and my kid brother lived just a block away. For the next five years we would continue moving about the Village and Cabbagetown, oddly always within a block or two of each other.

I'd landed my massage therapist position at the Fairmont Royal York Hotel's health club after a cold call to the manager. The hotel's neon-red sign has been part of the Toronto skyline for decades. Since I was a kid, that sign had signified immense wealth and a storied hotel where one day, if I was really lucky, I'd be able to stay. I never anticipated working at the Royal. I was still writing erotica (all of my fictional characters shared a surprising likeness to Kim), but the anthologies my stories appeared in got tighter with their payouts—like fifty dollars a story and two free copies. Erotica writing wasn't a sustainable career choice, so working as a massage therapist financed my predilection for fine reds, expensive running shoes and whimsical things like a seventy-dollar spice rack from Wildly Delicious that looked like a laboratory test-tube rack.

Having my own apartment was sovereignty at its finest. My landlord said I could choose any paint colour I wanted (within reason—and only one colour) and he would have the place painted for me within a month. I opted for a moody blue, a Sarah McLachlan–like winter sky, to reflect my emotional geography. He had it painted as promised; the painters sprayed right overtop of all the outlets, switch plates and the country crock chicken border that was plastered around the kitchen. My parents helped me out by financing a faux-leather black couch and armchair. My mom set me up with a fully kitted kitchen, with a zester, strainers, pots, a small toaster oven—everything. I found a table, oatmeal-coloured Parsons chairs and an espresso desk, and Ikea filled in all the other blanks. Kim, kind right until the end, bought me a TV to help me start out anew. She also made me a radiator cover so I could put a plant or some books on top of the rad. She kept collecting Air Miles on my extra account card for months, and it broke and warmed my heart at the same time. My life had been such a predictable pattern of Spirographs up until this point. I was desperate for the line that connected me to Kim to swirl and curve back already.

When I wasn't being such a sad sack, I hung out with a couple who owned a beagle that howled all the livelong day. Every Friday they'd have some friends over for test-tube shots. Eventually I brought the gang over to my place to show off my test-tube spice rack. My apartment soon became party central. I was one minute away from the previously famous girly bar Slack Alice, the Charles Khabouth of gay clubs, which was owned by Heather Mackenzie. She moved a few doors down and changed the moniker to Slack's. Friends would come to my place first; we'd crank up my impressive but invasive sound system, drink potent martinis and then head out, semi-sauced, to Slack's. Dax usually joined in—he loved the girl pack—and we often continued on after midnight to Fly, where the boys partied even longer, past dawn. I ended up meeting Andie again, the bright-eyed blonde who'd asked me years ago, "Why are you with that old lady?" I filled her in on the seven years and, more importantly, Kim. Andie knew Kim through another friend and wasn't surprised by my infatuation. *Everyone* loved Kim.

Dax and I hung out a lot during the week. It was cool having my bro right there in the city. We ran into each other on the street all the time, contrary to naysayers who claimed that Toronto is impersonal, too huge and full of strangers. He was living with his boyfriend, but he was always ready to check out a different coffee shop, take a long walk nowhere or simply open a bottle of wine and make dinner. Sometimes we'd tackle complicated recipes, inspired by the cooking classes we took at the Summerhill LCBO location. One night we made cold Thai salad rolls, until we discovered that rice paper is a bitch to work with, and our enthusiasm withered. While Dax and I had started out strong with perfect, elegant, tightly wrapped salad rolls of appropriate size, by the night's end we had Thai burritos as big as our arms, stuffing whatever we could into the rice paper, folding it crudely in half. Often, we'd comb through the back issues of the LCBO's *Food & Drink* magazines (an activity that consisted of me choosing things that I thought he should make for us) over Moscow Mules (ginger beer and vodka) or Old-Fashioned Whiskies.

It took a while, but I was getting into the groove of exercising both myself and my independence. I bought some canvas, painted my body and made instant art for my walls. I prepared proper things for dinner, even when Dax wasn't around. But despite my growing comfort with autonomy, I wished that Kim was sitting across from me. I kept her beloved mayonnaise, Cheez Whiz and a six-pack of Coors Light in my fridge, just in case she ever spontaneously dropped by again. A picture of her was propped up on the back of my toilet, strategically placed so I could see her sly smile when I looked in the mirror. In the photo she was leaning on the pool's edge at our resort in Holguin, and I was rather fond of teleporting myself back to Cuba and those halcyon days of just bikinis (or not) and mojitos with her.

I did end up with someone sitting across from me, eventually. Kelly perplexed a lot of my friends (and me, sometimes)—she wasn't my "type" at all. Kelly was a year younger than me and spent inordinate amounts of time on her hair and makeup. She loved pink velour and white rabbit-fur jackets and definitely turned heads wherever she went. I soon learned that Kelly spent 75 percent of her earnings on that pink prettiness. She loved everything retail—and eventually found a book series that consumed her, Sophie Kinsella's *Shopaholic*. Name a clothing store, and she had worked there. She had the best product lineup, from body wash that smelled like a vanilla milkshake to tingly Lip Venom gloss. She was a former cheerleader with a tight and toned body that she didn't mind showcasing in skinny jeans and tight tees. Kelly had been a gymnast too—she could walk out of the bar on her hands and then lower herself into the splits. I'd always been with older women who were androgynous, more phys. ed. teacher and steel-mill butch. So, Kelly was a big surprise all around. She obviously shook up my "type" setting. Though, if you were to line up all my exes in a group photo, there would be serious confusion. Curling team? People who met on a bus trip in Arizona? I liked that Kelly was so different from anyone else. This is why everyone was perplexed. Kelly was so opposite of all the girls I'd loved before, from the butch bravado of Dienne to Sandy, the motorcycle mama with Rod Stewart hair, to Sue, the stereotypically but permanently track-suited PE teacher, to Kim (who was perfect).

Kelly taught me a lot—like, did you know there's actually a size 0 for jeans? That's what she wore. I was a size 32. How can one person be a size 0 and the other a 32? She also introduced me to Black Entertainment Television and reality TV, specifically Nick Lachey and Jessica Simpson's riveting show, *Newlyweds*.

My family loved Kelly (I had to wonder if it was just because she wasn't Sue); my dad felt he was shaking hands with someone from *Melrose Place* when he first met her, and Dax liked her hyper-fun ways. She was highly animated when she spoke and knew how to have a good time with whatever or whoever was on hand.

While all this was going on, my apartment in the Village sat empty and my only tropical plant died due to neglect. I paid for cable TV that I never watched and for an apartment that I was no longer in. However, whenever Kelly and I did stop in to pick up my mail, she'd say, "I think it's about time you took this picture of your ex-girlfriend on the back of the toilet down." (But I didn't, not right away.)

And then, reluctantly, nine months later, I took Kim's picture down, gave my notice and moved my things a few blocks east to Kelly's six-hundred-square-foot apartment in Cabbagetown. My favourite part of the apartment was Gnu the cat. Gnu reminded me of Cypress, Rick's shoebox cat, but a short-haired version. I hated living in the high-rise, though. The elevator waits. The paid laundry thing in the basement—and the bratty kids who turned the laundry room into a playground, opening washers mid-cycle and dryer doors for fun. I hated that there was only a forty-five-minute window of sun on our south-facing balcony (nearby high-rises would blot it out in all other positions). Netting had to be put up to prevent a roost of ten thousand pigeons from settling in. I stared at my new world through what looked like a huge badminton net, missing Kim like crazy, even though I was with somebody else. I realized that Kim might never leave my head, so at some point, I decided to play along like everything was cool and I was well-adjusted. Moving to Cabbagetown was easy enough. Moving on was the bitch.

I picked up another part-time spa job massaging at the reputable King Edward Hotel. While I was free to roam at the Royal York if I didn't have a client, at this spa I had to quietly sit and wait. So I drank gallons of the lemon and honey tea that was intended for guests, and I wrote. I wasn't paid if I wasn't massaging, but I was also expected to sit and be ready to fly into action. Massage therapy was losing its zest, quickly. It was, in some ways, the perfect conduit for me, as it was portable and physical, but I was teetering on the edge of boredom. I wanted to do something more creative. My mom always said, "Only boring people get bored." I didn't want to be boring. So, I enrolled in evening writing classes at George Brown College.

And then the SARS (severe acute respiratory syndrome) breakout of 2003 slammed Toronto hotels. There had been forty-four deaths in the city related to SARS. Hotel occupancy was at an all-time low, and people didn't want to ride on the subway with coughing strangers, let alone get a massage. Both hotel bosses let me off the hook, and I found the reliable lift that writing always brings—so much so that even after the classes had ended, I continued not working some shifts, pretending that I was still "dashing off to school!"

The bonus and unfortunate thing about massage therapy is (not just Enya and her "Orinoco Flow") that you have *a lot* of uninterrupted time to think. I was thinking way too much and collecting inspirational quotes as if they were biblical passages. I had developed my own dream team of mentors, right down to Yoda:

"Train yourself to let go of everything you fear to lose." —Yoda

"Let life happen to you. Believe me: life is in the right, always."
—Rilke

"I'm living so far beyond my income that we may almost be
said to be living apart." —E.E. Cummings

"There is no greater agony than bearing an untold story inside
you." —Maya Angelou

As I tanned my stomach for forty-five minutes on the
Parliament Street high-rise balcony, I wrote, as Maya suggested.
I had agony and wanted to get to the rock bottom of it. What's
the formula for happiness? Is it where you live? Where you
work? Who you love? Do you need an equal percentile in each of
these things? Can one override them all? Was my happiest work
feeding the ferret and cleaning turtle tanks at the nature centre?
Or drawing Moker on her snowmobile? I didn't feel at home;
everything about the high-rise started to chisel at my well-being.
I was restless again and feeling stuck. I wanted to be back in my
brownstone with just my stuff.

I came home early from the hotel one night and Kelly was making
two elaborate sandwiches in the kitchen, neatly wrapping them in
saran. I was shocked—this was a rare moment, and my agitation
for the building and for living in the seedier part of Cabbagetown
lifted for a moment. I gushed thanks and really couldn't believe
it. She was making my lunch? This never happened, ever. I soon
learned that the lunch wasn't for me at all—it was lunch for some
guy at her workplace. I had spent the last few weeks trying to play it

cool about her getting picked up at work by some stone butch chick on a motorcycle. She had recently stopped answering her cellphone when I called from the hotel on my break. A pattern had developed where Kelly would meet her best friend from out of town to hit the bars, and sometimes she wouldn't come home for the entire weekend. I put my brain and heart on cruise control and wished that I could just shuffle my stuff back to my old apartment.

It was my existential crisis. I was now twenty-nine. So I decided I'd go solo to the Galapagos Islands for my thirtieth birthday to stay true to myself. Every single speech I did in elementary school had been on the Galapagos and Darwin and the blue-footed boobies. I wanted to see the frigate birds and vampire finches and Lonesome George, the centenarian tortoise. I wanted to see in person everything I had pawed over in Nan Chapin's *National Geographic* magazines. I wanted to smell that acrid bird guano deep in my nose, eat guinea pig (the Ecuadorian staple) and climb into lava tubes. Going to the Galapagos would free up necessary space in my brain to dwell on what I really wanted and needed.

I couldn't send the superlative-dense postcards home fast enough. The fabled islands served a greater, unexpected purpose—they were a pinprick introduction to travel becoming a necessary current in my life, not just chatty chimera. I wanted to be known as the person that did the stuff they said they would do. I would go to the places I talked about. I promised myself to take all my dream trips from age thirty forward—solo if necessary. As the wind whipped across Bartolomé's barren topography and threatened to lift the ball cap off my head, I trained my camera lens on the setting sun. I was beginning to fill the pages of my life with the content I wanted.

When I came back, I promptly moved out of that high-rise apartment building to another sweet brownstone on Earl Street, a block from where I originally started. I found Kim's poolside picture, placed it on the back of my toilet and said, "Hi." Kelly moved on to making lunches full-time for her six-foot-six beau. She was switching teams.

A few weeks later, I cautiously joined Pink Sofa, an online site for gay women, hoping to find a mate in New Zealand. That would solve things, I figured. Maybe I was done with Toronto—it *was* where you lived that mattered! I poured a stiff gin and tonic, scrolled through the Wharekauri, New Zealand, prospects and found one smiling face of interest. I sent off an introductory note to "Sims," boasting about how urban and cool I was.

11.

The Raspberry Capital of Canada

SOUNDTRACK: "GO WEST" by the Pet Shop Boys (yes, again).

There wasn't a lot of weight behind my online pursuit of Sims. She was a fun distraction, and I liked thinking about what her day, a day in New Zealand, might look like. Pink Sofa was a safe and harmless outlet for swapping anecdotal stories and flirting. But would I really move to New Zealand, or was this all just a waste of everyone's time? I liked the concept of New Zealand, what little I knew: cheap kiwi fruit, kiwi birds, regattas, manuka honey, rugby. But moving there was just a lark. Sims wasn't willing to waste precious dating time on a noncommittal Canadian who was just biding time. She called me out and our correspondence came to a polite end.

I was all over the map (literally and physically). Massaging at fancy spas had lost its zeal, and my search for anything stimulating and hopefully fulfilling jumped from Sims to chocolate making. I applied for a job as a chocolate maker in Streetsville. The shop was neat—they made truffles and chocolate-dipped pretzels and licorice in an old fire hall. I wasn't even that crazy about chocolate, but I could appreciate the artistry and sweet alchemy of gold dust and pinches of coconut. This application made about as much sense as scrolling through personal ads from New Zealand. Despite sending a mile-long essay about my life so far and how I was a bored massage therapist looking for a huge career jump into chocolate making, I was "rejected" again, probably for the same reason I was rejected by Sims: I wanted stuff without any effort. Soon I was on to becoming a cheesemonger or earning a Baking Arts certificate.

This is the problem when you have too many interests. While boring people may get bored, people interested in lots of things get interested in so many directions that it's almost impossible to choose a focus. I had to adjust my sails.

A few weeks after Sims disconnected my half-hearted advances from halfway around the world, "love" arrived in a police uniform. Let's call her Cagney so I can't be arrested. I met Cagney in the gym at the Royal York Hotel during my break; she was attending a police conference that the Royal was hosting. I was spinning on a bike, absently watching MuchMusic videos and eating a protein bar between clients. I noticed her immediately and knew that she was a sister. I didn't know that she was a cop, but she stacked enough plates on the leg-press machine to suggest that she did something physical for work. I kept spinning even though my bike's thirty-minute countdown had expired. I could see her in my peripheral, moving to the free weights, where she worked on her deltoids and triceps. I had a massage client booked in fifteen minutes, and I jumped off my bike just as she threw a towel over her shoulder and headed to the locker room.

The change room was jammed, and Cagney's locker was right beside mine. We shared flushed smiles and casually chatted. She said she was at the cop conference. "Are you attending it too?" I held up my uniform shirt with the Fairmont crest and said I worked at the hotel and had a massage appointment to get to. Neither of us disrobed, politely and patiently waiting for someone to make a move, preferably out of the locker room. The interest was mutual and palpable, so we exchanged numbers. I looked at the area code and asked where Cagney was from. "Abbotsford." I'd never heard of it and assumed it was in Ontario. When she said BC, something triggered. I'd soon learn that Abbotsford is known as the "city in the country" and is the Raspberry Capital of Canada.

Cagney said she made the best grilled maple salmon—she'd prove it to me—and she liked to bike too. She was training for a six-hundred-kilometre Cops for Canter fundraising ride, actually.

I hopped onto my own fantasy ride rather quickly, imagining life in BC. She had two dogs, and she introduced me to them via pictures on her phone—Bently was the golden retriever and Mila a white Lab. I would later learn that Mila technically belonged to Gillian, who rented the lower flat of Cagney's house. But both dogs were unaware of who owned whom and moved about the house freely. I admired Cagney's boldness, cop-ness, confidence and BC-ness immediately. We talked on the phone for three hours straight that night.

Cagney's conference was over the next day, but we arranged to meet for Thai food on Yonge Street just to see if we were still on the same wavelength. Conversation came easily. Maybe it was the time constraint we were working under, but we swapped important details first and everything escalated. "Come visit me," she suggested over green mango salad. It seemed laughable at first— I hadn't even known Cagney for twenty-four hours and she wanted me to come visit? "Stay for a week. Just give me the dates and I'll buy your ticket." And she did.

We flew back and forth for a few months, eating and seeing the very best bits of each other's province to learn more. Many hours were logged on the phone and in emails. With each trip, I left a few items behind, convinced that I would return and make a go of it. After several months of back and forthing, Cagney suggested that I should just move in already.

It was August—the same month in which I had moved to Vancouver in 1993. I was so hopeful and loved this fresh-slate state of being. Mila and Bently had both been to the groomer and were shampooed and toenail-trimmed, with cute bandanas knotted around their necks for the big day. "We're a family now, guys," Cagney told the dogs. She poured wine for me (not her) and served her famous maple salmon for dinner on the deck, as promised. It all seemed so promising.

But to work as an RMT in BC, I had to obtain a conditional licence and enrol in school again. I knew this prior to moving in with Cagney, but it quickly compounded my jadedness with the massage therapy industry. As an Ontario Registered Massage Therapist who graduated from a twenty-two-hundred-hour Massage Therapy Diploma program, I was required to go back to school to meet the British Columbia standard requirements for therapists (a three-thousand-hour diploma program). I'd been a bona fide therapist since 1999. With seven years in the field, I felt expert enough and totally unenthusiastic about logging eight hundred more hours, taking classes on "actinotherapy" (whatever that was), visceral manipulation (mobilizing stomachs and livers) and craniosacral therapy. Here I was in a profession that is designed entirely around relaxation, and I was a stress ball ready to implode.

I thought love would save the day and overshadow the nuisance of returning to school. I thought a life with dogs and a mountain peak in the distance would be the best thing yet. I was now part of a family and had to act the part. I took several buses and trains to the massage school in New Westminster, drank bucket-sized ten-dollar lattes from Starbucks to stay alert and endured liver-moving techniques. On top of all this, I had to pass the BC board exam to ensure that I was competent and suitable as a massage therapist in BC. And pay thousands of dollars to the school. I could barely work, as I was always commuting to take the silly courses. Solace was found in taking more courses—writing courses, not massage-related ones.

I was nervous to sign up for a three-year program at Douglas College, also in New Westminster, though it was exactly the program I had been looking for. Print Futures was a professional writing program that taught the foundations of writing and editing, but I was concerned about the length of the course; my sense of home and relationship were unstable, and it was hard for me to envision where I'd be in three years. I didn't trust my commitment to Cagney and to BC. The ghost of Kim kept me on edge. Yet this program was everything I would have wanted at a different time with somebody else in my life. The course piqued my interest like nothing before had: writing technical manuals, research reporting, writing for the web, public relations, magazines and trade publications. I applied and was narrowly accepted. Thankfully, the program administrator appreciated my humour; in addition to the typical personality questions and a multiple-choice section on grammar, I also had to provide explanations for several terms like "independent clause." Independent clause? I'd missed most of my grade thirteen English classes, so I wrote: "An independent clause would be best defined by Mrs. Clause on Christmas Eve."

I'd been in Abbotsford for six months and tried to ignore the niggling feeling that it wouldn't be long-term. Cagney was on to me (probably due to her sharp detective skills). "Are we just room-mates now, or what?" When I ordered her a tea with two sugars in it from Tim Hortons, she just about lost it. She never took two sugars; how did I not know or *care* to remember that? Our relation-ship had happened at cyclone speed, and now that I had moved to BC I felt stuck. A relationship refund wouldn't be easy. I should have moved to BC on my own accord, not with the framework of a relationship in the mix. But I knew I wouldn't have moved to BC otherwise, not with the demands of the massage college. Was I just in love with the idea of being away? Any good detective should have detected that.

As much as I wanted to delve into Print Futures and their promise of cool co-op terms at local newspapers and publishing houses, I signed up for only three courses. This temporarily revived me from the doldrums of the massage courses that drained my coffee cup and lifeblood. I ran between the campuses and wrote feverishly on the buses and train back to Mission (a two-and-a-half-hour ordeal), where I'd still have a twenty-minute drive "home" from the train station. I was the only non-full-time Print Futures student jumping into second-year classes to learn about the art of writing for magazines. I ate it up. In this class there was an emphasis on writing about what you knew; if you weren't a SME (subject matter expert), your writing would come off as hollow. "Marry your passions," our instructor, Joe Wiebe, advised us.

One week, he invited the *Vancouver Sun* books editor to our class to talk about the reality of the biz and what she expected from book reviews. "If you're interested, make your face known to me," Rebecca Wigod suggested. I made myself known and a week later was at the *Vancouver Sun* headquarters, eager to write reviews. Her desk was more like a fort built out of books, stacks and stacks of hardcovers and softcovers. She dug for some under her desk, emerged without missing a beat, handed me a few titles and then let me have a go at the rest of the piles. "Find a few that appeal to you and then we'll talk about a deadline." I grabbed five books and we talked deadlines and word counts and payment. I couldn't believe I could earn two hundred dollars reading a book!

I was working (barely, due to school commitments and commuting) on a conditional licence from the BC College of Massage Therapists. I'd have to write the BC board exam in a few months, but the licence permitted me to work during the transition period. In addition to massaging at a spa in Abbotsford, I tried my hand at copy writing job ads and adverts for Valentine's Day and Mother's Day. This I loved!

It was time for an epiphany, and it came in the form of a tattoo on my right deltoid: a striped hot-air balloon with a tiny anchor suspended below the balloon instead of a basket. If you have any tattoos, you already know what comes next: "What does it mean?" I didn't realize what my balloon and anchor meant at the time, but I loved the image. I'd been carrying around a clipping with the image for so many years that I no longer remembered what band had the hot-air balloon on their album cover.

A sixty-something, spritely British woman named Gillian was living downstairs from us at that time. We would get together and drink pots and pots of Earl Grey tea and talk about four things ad nauseum: Oprah, dreams, horoscopes and Sylvia Browne, a psychic medium. Gillian had her own psychic tendencies and was keen to decipher all my dreams. I was having repetitive ones about snakes, a symbol of transformation, and hummingbirds, a symbol of restlessness. Though she wasn't a fan of tattoos, Gillian was curious about my hot-air balloon. I explained it with an Oprah theory tied in: as Oprah had said, if you imagined your life as a hot-air balloon ride, too many sandbags in the basket would prevent you from getting off the ground; to really achieve your potential, you had to cut your sandbags. The fewer sandbags you carried around, the higher you would soar. And oh—the view from that spot in the sky! Sandbags could take the form of several things: needy friends, needier exes, draining family members, taxing jobs, demanding children or the weight of secrets and disappointments. I counted my career as a massage therapist as a sandbag: a big dead weight that was holding me down.

I tried this theory out with Gillian, who spun it around even better, as she always did. She poured more tea and said, "But don't you think it has been your anchor too? Keeping you grounded? A sandbag or an anchor doesn't have to be a negative thing."

By God, she was right. Gillian knew I was untethered already and ready to set sail again. This is what I needed to do, desperately.

That night I thought about Joe's class. All I had to do was marry my passions. I had so many, but I thought of Jane Goodall first and keyed her name into the computer. I read the "About" section of the Jane Goodall Institute (JGI) and didn't hesitate to click on "JOBS AT JGI." There was a posting for a Roots & Shoots coordinator in Uganda. Uganda? I didn't even know where that was. I knew a bit about Roots & Shoots, about how it was designed to empower youth with community projects, leadership opportunities and environmental awareness. It was a volunteer position, writing curriculum for local programs in conjunction with teachers— programs that focused on the connections between community, health, the environment and Uganda's wildlife. Total expert on this.

As I filled out the application, I leaned back on my nature centre experience, upselling my curriculum design from ten years ago. I bragged about my Print Futures experience and my early portfolio chronicling Moker the cat on her snowmobile. I could write curricula about chimpanzees and building wells. I'd dug one in Costa Rica with my bare hands. My head was apparently in a hot-air balloon.

I had just passed the BC board exam to be a full-fledged massage therapist in BC. It was a lacklustre achievement. I had been funnelling all my energy into book reviews for the *Vancouver Sun* and Oprah theories. I looked at the hot-air balloon inked into my deltoid. The good thing about anchors is that you can pull them up and throw them overboard somewhere else.

I filled out the necessary forms while Cagney slept. Bently made his rounds a few times, making sure I wasn't having any secret snacks without him. I imagined my new life in Uganda (once I had Googled its location). I was channelling Karen Blixen—maybe I'd procure a coffee plantation while I was there. Bently sighed and flopped down at my feet. His brown eyes were like a tattoo gun on my heart. If he could talk, he would tell me that he was terribly disappointed in me. What about our daily runs? I told him that I *might* be going to Africa, but I'd be back. I wouldn't forget him, and we'd be running our usual route along Clayburn Creek in no time. I planned to investigate the stickier details of my plan later—like flights, immunizations, malaria. Quitting my spa job. Telling my *girlfriend* that I had applied for a job in Uganda.

Deep down I knew I was wholly unqualified, but recalling CBC anchor Peter Mansbridge's story buoyed me. In his early days, working as a clerk at an airport in Manitoba, a flight announcer had called in sick. With no short-notice replacement available, the supervisor asked Mansbridge to announce a delayed flight. A local radio station manager heard his voice and recruited Mansbridge to come work at his station on the spot. Peter Mansbridge was sent to CBC Radio's northern service shortly thereafter. This is how things happen.

It was May and the JGI position didn't start until July. I was so preoccupied with my potential Uganda relocation that I floated through the days, neither here nor there. I'd take Bently out for runs and then come back for Mila, Gillian's adorable white Labrador, who apparently didn't believe in heavy cardio. One day, Bently and I hit the road, taking side streets to the creek. I spun my iPod Nano to "Africa" by Toto, my new theme song. I had my earbuds in and went from the Raspberry Capital of Canada to East Africa in a few steps. Bently pulled like a wild stallion as he usually did, and I rolled my eyes when I heard the catcalls and whistles of a construction crew over Toto's lyrics. So annoying.

But then I looked ahead and saw what all the whistling was about. I was so absorbed in Africa that I failed to notice the just-poured cement sidewalk that Bently had mounted onto. I was about to follow him— Bently was knee-deep in cement! I tugged him out, embarrassed, as cinder blocks quickly formed on poor Bently's feet. We ran down to Mackenzie Creek, where I let him swim, then I kneeled at the bank to rinse off the evidence. I shook Africa out of my head for a little while.

I hadn't heard anything from Jane Goodall by mid-June and assumed the position had been filled, rightfully by someone skilled. I bought a plane ticket "home" to regroup in Toronto for two weeks in July. If Uganda wasn't in the cards, I needed something new to cling to. Maybe a good dose of friends and family would balance me again. Everyone would be in town for Pride, and I needed to recalibrate. I had a long list of my favourite haunts to revisit for coffee, pints and jerk chicken.

The morning I was to fly to Toronto, I received an email from Jane Goodall. Not from her personally, but from one of her staff at JGI Entebbe. I didn't get the job I had applied for, but there was a new posting that my skill set was better suited for. Would I be interested in editing a book on the tribes and totems of Uganda? As soon as possible?

Of course.

12.
Flight Risk: Uganda

"You'll be totally income neutral for four months. What's to worry about?" my brother said, clinking his champagne flute against mine.

There were plenty of things to worry about: fizzling relationship dynamics, asking for a sabbatical from the spa (or having to quit), obtaining a Ugandan visa, yellow fever and typhoid immunizations and making mortgage payments while I was volunteering. Income neutral wasn't so neutral when the expenses started rolling in. Paying half of the monthly mortgage while I was in Africa volunteering was Cagney's secret way of punishing me—or that's how I interpreted it. Not that I was expecting a free ride, but maybe she could have cut me a little slack considering her substantial cop salary? She couldn't comprehend why I'd pay exorbitant amounts to volunteer in Africa when I could do good in our own community. She didn't get why I wanted to help chimpanzees rather than starving children. Cagney pointed out that the fact that I was willing to spend $2,580.14 on a flight from Vancouver to Amsterdam to Entebbe, Uganda, meant I definitely had enough money to still contribute to the mortgage. Some of her points were reasonable, but everything else sounded like dream squashing to my ears. While the average human being could understand the practicality of her questioning, I heard nothing but unsupportiveness for my mission. When I apologized and blamed it on restlessness and a need to do something creatively challenging, things turned sour.

"You don't get to like everything you do in life," said Cagney. "You have to take responsibility at some point, not just fly off to the jungle or Africa when you're bored."

I suppose this was reasonable too, but I still don't agree. I think you should be able to like everything you do in life, and if you don't, for God's sake, change it. In the heat of the moment, I quoted Rita Mae Brown out loud: "I finally figured out the only reason to be alive is to enjoy it."

Even if it cost $2,580.14 for a flight to get me there.

I've always felt like I've been playing a crazy game of Monopoly. For what little money I made as a massage therapist, in the grand scheme of things (due to my own self-imposed rules of working only four days a week, five massages a day, maximum), I still could afford to pay for flights, whether to the Galapagos or Costa Rica.

This is what "income neutral" would come to mean:

- $2,580.14 for return airfare from Vancouver, BC, to Entebbe, Uganda
- $525.69 for anti-malaria pills
- $185.00 for a consultation with a travel doctor and a yellow fever and typhoid shot
- $155.65 for Dukoral and more Malarone (anti-malaria pills)

- $110.00 US for a Ugandan visa with a three-month extension
- $614.74 for a Toshiba Satellite laptop
- $50.38 for a 100-watt adapter plug
- $34.60 for a copy of *Lonely Planet East Africa*
- $27.85 for insect repellent, whistle, match case and emergency blanket, as suggested by JGI
- $62.82 for a 2G memory card, 4G memory stick, toothpaste, body butter, SPF, floss, Q-tips, envelopes and flip-flops
- $325.60 for travel insurance that would basically be void in all the times I would need it due to acts of God, natural disasters, conflicts and uprisings
- $2,400.00 for mortgage payments

And a whole lot more: passport and visa photos, blank journal, a four-month tampon cache, quick-dry shorts and an alarm clock.

Total: priceless.

Yeah, it's not cheap to volunteer. I was also asked to pay six hundred dollars US for accommodations at the Jane Goodall Institute office, which was on the upper floor of a proper house. Lunch would be included. I negotiated a fair deal and traded my brand-new laptop for a single bed and a mozzie net, as JGI was in desperate need of another one for the office.

If you've followed the bouncing ball along this far, you may have come to your own conclusions—that is, that I was clearly a flight risk. Africa had been a latent dream for me, one hatched long ago in Nan's library of *Nat Geos*, but it had never seemed feasible. Had I not been sitting in Joe's magazine writing class, the connection might have been lost. "You need to marry your passions."

I do.

The power went out five minutes after I landed at Entebbe International Airport. It was an indication of things to come. I hadn't heard from the Roots & Shoots coordinator for two weeks. Our last correspondence was her reply to my request for a few photos of the JGI house. I was having lucid flashbacks of my patchy dealings with Daniel when he said I could sleep on his couch and he'd find a job for me at *Cockroach*. I wanted a few visuals to go along with my merry *Out of Africa* savannah soundtrack—knowing I'd have some real cockroaches to contend with too. She had sent a close-up picture of a single bed, empty shelves (my dresser) and something that was blurry and upside down. That was it. There were no details about who might meet me at the airport or a specific address if I was to hail a taxi and arrive on my own. The details were even looser than the ones I clung to when I'd moved out to Vancouver. But I went with this positive affirmation: If someone doesn't meet me, I'll get a cab. Surely Entebbe isn't that big, and the taxi driver will know of the very famous Jane Goodall office, for sure.

Once the baggage carousel heaved to life again with a return-of-power surge, I was thrilled to see my backpack. There was a crush of Ugandans waiting for family members and lots of homemade signs.

Missionaries hugged other missionaries and UN workers found their kin. I was the last woman standing. Ten persistent cabbies were eager to give me a ride. I decided to wait it out for a bit, and eventually, a woman with a wild tousle of grey hair hurried in and grabbed me. We both knew without introductions that we belonged to each other.

Carol was one of the JGI staffers from Boston. She filled in the gaps for me about life at "the Chimp House," where a small army of dogs howled us in at the manned barbed-wire gate of the office.

"We have a problem with these gatehouse guys sleeping instead of guarding, so just be aware of your surroundings," said Carol.

I immediately made fast friends with Levi (a Rhodesian mix), Scrappy (a typical fox-like street dog) and Tinker, a gorgeous black Lab who was all tongue. There were two tan pups—Beavis and Rasta, an orange tabby named Juwa, and a knock-off of Moker, Pops, who did tight figure eights around my ankles.

Carol breezed me through the house. We'd be the only ones there for a few nights, as Jacquie, the Roots & Shoots coordinator, was in Northern Uganda on a project, and my other future house-mates were in Budongo and Murchison. It was a running roll call of dogs, cats, places and notable names that I tried to embed in my jet-lagged head. "We have an honour system here, a running tab—so, there's always cold beer and pop in the fridge; just mark down when you take one." Gosh, how civilized. That was easy to make note of.

Despite jet lag and crampy legs from such a long haul, I was immediately energized. Landing at night meant the drive from the airport to the Chimp House, just five kilometres away, was a blur of bikes, horns, heat and kerosene lanterns. The air was sweet with wood-fire smoke and I felt at home, just like that. Carol apologized that she had paperwork to tend to but promised to take me to the night market on Tuesday. "You have to get the Rolex. Trust me." (And she did take me, as promised, before she headed back to the States. The Rolex—a mix of chopped tomato, purple onions and cabbage rolled in a fluffy omelette—is rumoured to have been a misinterpretation of "Rolled Eggs." As vendors called out their wares, "Rolled Eggs" sounded like "Rolex.")

I helped myself to a big Nile Special from the fridge (beer in Uganda comes in a realistically sized 750-millilitre bottle) and started my tally sheet with a happy tick.

Upstairs, with the cats sniffing out the foreign scent of Mila and Bently, I set up camp. The photos that Jacquie had sent were true to life—here was the single bed with a knotted-up mosquito net and a pseudo dresser. I swept up some dead cockroaches. *Cockroach!* Oh, how far I'd come. I emptied five books out of my pack (one of which I had already read on the ten-hour flight from Amsterdam— *The Poisonwood Bible*). Prior to leaving, I only allowed myself to read Africa books. It was my own self-imposed course on culture, fauna, history and Jane. I'd jumped from Jane Rule to Jane Goodall. I read every memoir and guidebook available at the local library branch in Abbotsford.

Waiting for morning and the grand reveal of Uganda in resplendent African sunlight was near torture. While I waited, I added to my journal all sorts of pithy observations from Amsterdam, where I had a brief four-hour layover just half a day ago. I had decided to sneak into the city on the efficient train from Schiphol Airport to Centraal Station. I had one destination in mind: Hotel Titus, Leidsekade 74, on the Marnixstraat Canal. I wasn't staying there— no, I was just revisiting my ghosts. Kim and I had spent a week there in 2002. We had sat in the enormous window of Hotel Titus, watching the world float by on the canal, daydreaming, as we were prone to doing. We had moved the king-size bed closer to the window and butted it up against the sill so we could lie in bed and still take in the view.

Kim was omnipresent, even in Africa. When I should have been thinking of Cagney, I was writing letters in my head to Kim. I thought of her at dawn, her alarm sounding off at 4:30 a.m. for another shift at the steel mill. She'd be freaked out to learn that my African alarm wasn't cheery birdsong—it was bats. Just before the sun turned the sky cotton-candy pink, a hundred bats filtered through a narrow passage in the roof and into the attic above my

Chimp House bedroom. The flurry of activity was unsettling in the fog of jet lag. This was a routine thing. At sunset the bats did the reverse, spilling out into the sky in a black oblong cloud. It was a new way of telling the time for me.

Around 2:00 a.m. the winds would start up, whipping fiercely off the surface of nearby Lake Victoria. The gusts would turn wet, with rain hammering the window and the side of the Chimp House with an intensity that I'd never felt. It rained nearly every day in Abbotsford, but not angrily like this. At about 2:45 the lightning show would begin with hot, white bolts dividing the sky. And then the thunder, vibrating the ground and my bones. I felt like I was six years old all over again, shaking away, waiting for the next blow. The lightning strikes on Lake Victoria actually make the official top 500 lightning spots list. Apparently, central Africa has 283 of the world's top 500 sites. Those storms would roll in, night after night. Trees bent in half, palm fronds scratched the roof—and the thunder blasts were like close-range cannons. The house shook and vibrated and the earth sounded like it was going to shear in half. All the animals found refuge in my bed. I was thrilled to have them all packed in with me, mosquito net askew, not really doing its protective work, as one of the cats ripped a hole for easier access to the nestled company. The storm would lash out for an incredible, wide-eyed hour and then blow on. Finally, my bed of four or seven beasts could rest.

But there's no rest for the weary. With the first suggestion of sunrise, vervet monkeys were squeaking in the trees. Marabou storks were *skwonking*. Pied crows in their tidy white vests cawed even louder. Sunbirds, white-browed robin chats, rollers, weavers and fire finches all joined in on the morning singsong. It was electric.

Days went like this: Signature thunderstorm from two until four in the morning, followed by hot-as-hell tea and bread as heavy as a brick from the local bakery (spread with "groundnut paste," which is peanut butter in its most natural form). A five-kilometre run down to Anderita Beach and back, smiling at the women with woven baskets full of shiny fish on their heads. Usually I'd have a few tagalongs, kids or adults, barefoot or in flip-flops, taunting me from ahead, or running behind me as a dare.

I'd drift down to the office after a shower, with more hot tea in hand, and settle down to my project: a stack of more than five hundred drawings and stories from local schoolchildren about Ugandan totems and tribes. My role was to edit the cultural compendium, which would be distributed to Ugandan schools involved in the Roots & Shoots program. It was all-absorbing, and I'd pester Jacquie every few minutes by holding up a darling doodle of a crazy-eyed lion or a hyena with three legs. This was good, nourishing work. Scrappy laid at my feet, and the birdsong seemed piped in. I was in shorts and mildly perspiring—my two favourite things. We'd break and head outside with plates of mashed plantain, rice, sweet potatoes (oh yeah, hello starch!) and savoury stewed goat.

After work, I'd take off down to the marina or the beach again, stopping at all the tiny makeshift vendors along the way, who were selling Chiclets, cobs of corn, meticulously polished men's dress shoes, dried fish, freckled bananas, gas in plastic water bottles, sweets, and mangoes as big as footballs. I'd buy skewers of barbecued chicken and more goat and hurry back to the Chimp House before sundown. The next few hours I spent in sheer un-interrupted bliss, with a tall Bell beer and a book I found on the Chimp House shelves: *A House Somewhere: Tales of Life Abroad*. This was *my* house somewhere.

And then I met Merryde, the owner of the elegant Gately Inn boutique hotel, just up the road from the Chimp House. The staff at JGI all loved her, and drinks and lazy dinners at ambient Gately became habitual. Everything was carefully curated at the Gately, right down to the Australian wine list—a reflection of Merryde's roots and her other home, on the Sunshine Coast of Queensland, Australia. We connected immediately, and I found myself regularly wandering up to Gately for gin and tonics or Cobb salads to the din of crickets and Merryde's Aussie purr. Not only did Merryde have another house somewhere, she had another inn too—in Jinja, on the Nile.

This was somebody who was living her dreams out loud. Over the course of many bottles of wine under the chandelier of the African sky and spooky planetary alignments (the conjunction of Venus and Jupiter), the stories filtered out, back and forth, like breathing. As Merryde recounted the evolution of Gately on the Nile, it was proof that marrying passions is necessary. She had fallen for Africa in 1999. "I felt as if I had come home."

Despite enormous obstacles, local backlash, property battles and debilitating rounds of malaria, Merryde persevered with her un-swerving vision. She established a renowned restaurant (Pancakes Panache with bananas, roasted peanuts and honey! Golden, flaky beef samosas with red chili jam! Fiery Kashmiri chicken!). She designed a full Thai menu with the help of her Thai friend Nee, planted enviable gardens, constructed thatched *banda* cottages and curated rooms that felt, indeed, like home.

She was obviously someone I needed to latch on to, for good. If planets were aligning above our heads, I needed to align with like-minded people like Merryde who didn't think pursuing happi-ness was a privileged option for the irresponsible. Like Cagney did.

13.

Christmas on the Kazinga Channel

I HAD LATCHED ON TO a Rwandan proverb and made it my new mantra: "You can outdistance that which is running after you, but not what is running inside you."

I loved it all: the dusty roads the colour of paprika and the antics of the vervet monkeys in the tree canopies, trying to target passersby with pulpy mango pits. I loved the larger-than-life insects and the twittering colonies of weaver birds along Kampala Road that turned trees festive with their suspended globe-like nests swaying from the branches.

As much as the chronic horn-honking was an assault to my senses, I couldn't believe what passed by me on any given day. There were motorcycles balancing bunk beds, *boda bodas* (motorcycle taxis) carrying not only sidesaddle passengers, but also four-hundred-pound Nile perch. Women in brilliantly coloured dresses would ride past, laughing, holding live upside-down chickens or a small hog-tied bleating goat over their shoulders. A *boda boda* could carry five people and a car engine, no problem. Sinewy teen girls balanced flats of eggs stacked six high. Men in broken flip-flops pedalled rickety old ten-speeds along the gravel shoulder, dragging lengths of rebar or ten-foot rolls of corrugated steel. Beat-up pickup trucks cruised by, laden with sugar cane, cabbages and a dozen squatting locals with machetes, singing their heads off in the back. *Matatus* (minivan taxis) motored along, vibrating with gospel music or Michael Jackson's "Thriller." Vehicles that could safely seat five North Americans were used to transport twenty Ugandans. I counted all the arms and legs once, as I was stuffed in the back right-hand corner with someone's armpit in my nose, a jug of kerosene (not mine) between my feet and half a bag of charcoal and rice on my lap. Nobody wore helmets, though in Kampala, Uganda's capital city, I did see a few football helmets worn by *boda boda* drivers. One wore just the sponge insert from a helmet. All this traffic was boggling—especially with raw eggs, live goats, gigantic fish, and trucks belching along with loads of charcoal on the same shared route. Thriller, indeed.

I absorbed it all, made punch-drunk by the scenery. "Can you hear the smell?" I could. Body odour, diesel, rotting mangoes, arid land, the lake, the haze of oil lanterns, the charcoal embers of the Rolex stands, meat spitting on the grill, day-old beef hanging in a cloud of flies from hangers. I could hear all the smells.

Right down to the smell of fried insects in the microwave. Ruth, our beloved JGI cook, was an enormous fan, and I'd often buy her a sleeve of fried grasshoppers at the Tuesday night market. She liked her grasshoppers hot, so she'd throw the folded newspaper pouch into the micro before devouring them, like a post-pub-crawl feed of poutine. She'd offer a few to mewing Juwa, the ginger cat, who enjoyed grasshoppers as much as she liked offerings of goat from my take-away dinners. I became a big fan too—grasshoppers became my Tuesday staple. I'd walk to the market and find my favourite spot on a bench, where I'd grab a beer and patiently wait for the guy that walked around with a big plastic pail of grasshoppers. They were ten cents for a handful. I couldn't believe my life—transported into such a scene, eating grasshoppers and drinking beer in Uganda!

I tried to play down my love affair with Uganda for Cagney, whom I dutifully Skyped on Sunday nights, as agreed. She had cottoned on to the fact that I had found happiness. (It was *where* you lived! It was *what* you did for work! *Who* you loved didn't have to be part of the equation! I didn't mention that, of course.) "I think you're happy," said Cagney, "because you don't have any responsibilities there." I thought of the Van Gogh Museum in Amsterdam. When you walk through the gallery rooms and different decades of Van Gogh's life, you can see an obvious change in mood reflected in his palette. The bright, cheery sunflowers turn to moody blues and dark, hopeless scenes in no time. I wondered if my own personal gallery would appear like this: Abbotsford, one dark rain cloud; Uganda, unicorns and lollipops in the sun.

I was relishing responsibilities of *my* choosing. My schedule was designed by me—and what a design it was! Weekends were dedicated to exploring, poking around quirky markets full of rat traps, lacy underwear, soccer cleats, carrots and knock-off perfumes, and lazing about Anderita Beach with good books and half-finished letters home. I nursed beers until sundown, watching the buzz of activity on Lake Victoria as fishermen came and went, successful and not. I chatted with kid vendors selling roasted corn (starchy, like the cattle corn Nan Torti tried to feed us, but a Ugandan favourite) and tiny packets of red-skinned groundnuts. I'd order a grilled tilapia early on, as it took a while to actually appear (and you'd get the whole thing, eyeballs, tail and all), and think about

Rwandan proverbs. Nothing could be better than this: a broiling sun, some groundnuts and aimlessly watching wading hamerkops stride along the shore, seeking out tiny fish. Their bills and crests made their feathered heads look exactly like hammers.

I had plowed through the *Tribes and Totems of Uganda*, which I edited and collated in a month's time, despite having four months to complete the project. All my neurons were lit up by this new-found creative outlet. I was so energized by the shiny newness of a job that required doing exactly what I loved: reading. My only interruption was to grab more ginger tea from the kitchen or scratch the ears of Scrappy or Levi, who had come to lie at my feet. The electric pinch-me moments of "How is this my life?" never stopped. I had created my own alternate universe in Entebbe, Uganda.

It had been a learning curve. Totem poles in Canada act as symbols of a clan, family wealth and prestige. They are traditionally carved from tall cedar trees and tell of legends, clan lineage and notable events. There are more than seventy crest figures carved on North American totem poles, such as killer whale, beaver, frog, starfish and wolf. The word "totem" is derived from the Ojibway word *odoodem*, which means "his totem, his kinship." Among the Batooro, Banyoro and Baganda tribes in Uganda, more than a hundred plant and animal species are considered totems. A chief's furniture and other items are decorated with personal totems or those of the tribe. The duty of the community members is to protect and defend their totems. In some traditional African religions the belief is that when you die, you are reincarnated as the type of animal that your tribe regarded as their totem.

With over five hundred submissions from forty Ugandan primary schools, there was a lot to take in about the Lugbara clan and their leopard totem or the taboo of eating grasshoppers or lungs for female Omusiji tribe members; men were not allowed to eat sheep or liver. In the Abagaye clan, parents of the daughter to be married were to pay a dowry of cows and goats—*not* sheep and beer. Jacquie filled in some of the critical cultural blanks for me over our morning ginger teas and sugary roadside *mandazi* (a typical East African doughnut).

The taboos associated with sacred totem animals in Ugandan tribes were deeply instilled in the young Roots & Shoots club members. They shared their wide-eyed fear in stories that illustrated the consequences. If you tried to kill, harm or eat your totem animal, you would die all sorts of gruesome deaths. For the Mwiruntu, if you ate elephant meat, you could lose your manhood. For the Omusambu clan, whose totem is the *empindo* (weaving needle), eating from a newly made basket before washing it can result in losing all of your teeth. Respecting this taboo has helped conserve wetlands, as the Omusambu reuse old baskets instead of cutting more reeds.

Ugandan totems provide feathers for cultural ceremonies and also manure, which helps crops grow. They help eat pests and encourage tourism. The kids have learned, in turn, that poaching and clear-cutting forests for charcoal (a popular source for open-fire cooking) is detrimental to their culture's very foundation. They are a mighty force, these kids, recognizing early on that they need to save their totems. They already see the vital correlation of wildlife and the attraction it has become for tourists.

The project was fulfilling on so many fronts for me, so much so that I ripped through it and still had almost three months to go on my stint at JGI. Debby Cox (not to be confused with the Canadian R & B singer), the executive director and devout JGI staffer, asked if I could draw monkeys. I'd seen a vervet up close and personal on my birthday, when I wrestled my birthday cake away from him just outside the JGI office. I can still see his little menacing teeth chattering while his eyes darted between mine and the ultimate sweet prize in the plastic bag. "Monkeys? Sure, probably."

"Maybe you could do a colouring book for the Roots & Shoots kids, for JGI. And our partners at the Dian Fossey Foundation in Rwanda could make use of it too." I was now the designated, knighted, Chief Colouring Book Designer. See, I had responsibilities!

My days spun in a wonderful new direction, researching the primates of Uganda. Debby rightly gave me heck once over a preliminary drawing in which I had wrongly given a certain monkey a prehensile tail. I was dealing with Jane Goodall's next in line, so there were no errors to be made. Debby had an Order of Australia for her chimp-conservation efforts; her love of chimps and hatred for plastics were in equal amounts. But I adapted quite easily to drawing monkeys all day on the veranda of the Chimp House, happy to not be parked in front of my laptop, but with a sketch pad in hand instead.

Debby was also best mates with Merryde (both were Australian), so this meant even more nights up at Gately and animated conversations over the inn's signature savoury aubergine and feta stacks. We swirled Shiraz and stories until Merryde returned to Australia for her usual respite, leaving a palpable hole in my evenings.

The office was an ever-changing bunch. The Chimp House saw influxes in numbers and then quieter nights when it would be just Lou (another Aussie) and me. There was a solid stack of books, *Vanity Fair* mags and DVDs from volunteers past—we were working our way through it all. Kristy and Andrea, from Melbourne, camped out with us for a bit when the UN pulled them out of Goma and the chimp sanctuary they were working at. They came with Baileys, red velvet cake and a penchant for nachos made with Doritos chips.

The very handsome and appropriately named Kevin Danger arrived from New Zealand with a Polish carpenter who was going to help with some construction near an eco-lodge run in conjunction with JGI in the Budongo Forest Reserve. A videographer from the Discovery channel bunked with us for a few nights, and a photographer from California arrived next. Carol came back. Debby left. Jacquie went north. The Chimp House was a hotel of all sorts.

Thanks to Debby and her faith in my monkey-drawing skills, I ended up painting some wall murals in the Budongo eco-lodge cabins. (I had zoomed through the *ABC to Primates of Uganda* colouring book gig at breakneck speed.) I didn't need much convincing. "You can track the chimps when you're in Budongo too. You need to do that already. Sipi will take you out in the morning and then you can paint in the afternoons." The biodiversity at Budongo was startling: 9 different species of primates, 366 species of birds, 289 types of butterflies and 465 species of trees. It's one of the best-preserved and largest rainforests in East Africa.

Chimp tracking! Painting monkeys! I spent a week with my neck craned skyward, tramping around at dawn in wellies, watching the dynamics and antics of the chimp troop. They thumped the strangler-fig trunks in display, shared figs like lovers enjoying a romantic candlelit dinner and groomed each other with such affection. My life was becoming *National Geographic* pages in real time—FaceTime before it was invented. I took it all in—that musky smell that indicates the presence of chimps and the pesky, alarmist barking baboons (also indicating chimp presence). Sipi, one of Budongo's prized guides and trackers, loved the chimps, but he loved birds even more. He rhymed off so many species my head spun.

It was now nearly Christmas, and without getting too colonial, I wanted to introduce eggnog to my Ugandan JGI team. After being introduced to the Rolex, Stoney Tangawizi ginger beer and *mandazi*, I needed to share some authentic Canadiana. Eggs were never refrigerated (a Ugandan tradition), which was something I had to adjust to early on. However, with all the rolling blackouts, the fridge would often be out for three days at a time at the Chimp House, so what did it matter?

A few weeks prior, I'd been up late at night, weathering one of Entebbe's famous earth-shaker storms. I was prowling Facebook and thought, *Hey, I wonder if Jann Arden is on here?* I knew she had been in Ethiopia from a *Reader's Digest* article. I found Jann and her Fann club with a quick search and said I was in Uganda, volunteering with the Jane Goodall Institute, drawing monkeys, watching German *Rocky* movies and wondering what her time in Ethiopia was like. A response came back immediately, which was surprising given the dodgy African Wi-Fi. My late nights began to include passing notes back and forth with Jann. The timing was perfect. With the eleven-hour time-zone difference between Uganda and Vancouver, I was up after midnight having a gin, and she was already in the studio, drinking green tea, recording her album *Free*.

We got to talking about Christmas and how weird it was to be hot and without any Christmas feeling or decorations in Africa. (Most Ugandans go to the zoo on Christmas Day—this is *the* thing to do.) I said I wanted to make some eggnog because to me, Boney M and eggnog really round out the holiday, even if I was wearing flip-flops and watching monkeys outside my window. Jann fired back her foolproof recipe: Just blend a dozen egg yolks, a carton of cream and a cup of sugar. That was it. Oh, and add booze.

There was a lot of Waragi (Ugandan gin that tasted more like gasoline than juniper) around, but rum was a little more exotic. I found one dusty bottle of Captain Morgan dark rum in an East Indian–owned grocery store in Entebbe. It cost almost sixty dollars

US and probably travelled on five ships to get there, but I didn't balk. I bought a dozen still-warm brown eggs from the closest roadside stand and a carton of long-life cream and got in the true holiday spirit. If I killed off the entire Chimp House with eggnog, Jann Arden was going down with me. Everyone survived, though the Ugandans were cautious (despite their love of the potent and toxic-tasting Waragi). No one contracted salmonella, but they certainly questioned such a bizarre Canadian tradition. Drinking raw eggs with rum? Really? Gross. But pass the fried grasshoppers.

I had mixed emotions about the impending Christmas holidays and not enough rummy nog to numb my mounting anxiety. Cagney was to arrive on the twentieth, and two days later we were to go on a ten-day safari and then carry on to Kenya. I was tidying up the last of my work with JGI and missing it already. Let's just say that expression about absence making the heart grow fonder failed to resonate.

Lesson learned (now, not then): you don't have to go all the way to Africa to break up with someone, but sometimes you have to. Our recent Skype conversations had fallen flat and agitated me more than anything. I'd have to leave the beach early to get back to the JGI office in time to reach her before she left for work. I should have been thrilled to show her *my* Africa, but I felt like she was tainting it with a possibly justified but still negative attitude about my being there.

I paced at the Entebbe airport, my nerves frayed in the wrong way. I should have been ready to explode with excitement to see my girlfriend after being apart for so long. Trying to muster up enthusiasm when there's none is a nearly impossible feat. Especially when dealing with a detective who is trained to observe facial expressions and fidgeting behaviour. The doors to the baggage claim area opened and closed repeatedly with a parade of weary travellers. I saw her and felt…ready to throw up, more than anything. Our conversation in the cab back to the Chimp House quickly drifted from niceties to stilted. Cagney muttered (audibly), "I knew this was a bad idea."

I grabbed her a Coke from the kitchen (and a beer for me) before sitting awkwardly on the end of my single bed. Cagney valiantly attempted to reignite things. I felt nothing but irritation and validation that our relationship had long expired. She called me out on it immediately. "You just kissed me like I'm your favourite aunt." (I have never kissed any of my aunts remotely like that.) She was so convinced that we were over that she was willing to fly back to Canada the next day. Now there's a guilt trip! There was no yelling, just hot silence. We lay on the even hotter foam mattress like mannequins, refusing to touch. I was so pissed at her for ruining Uganda so quickly for me. But, in keeping with my wishy-washy nature, I persuaded Cagney to stay. She had just flown nineteen hours to be with me.

This predictable scene would be repeated on a daily basis. Ten days together in a stuffy Land Rover with a bunch of strangers from Germany didn't spell out romantic reconciliation. It ended up being a dramatic, emotional safari instead. One I was growing tired of. I had the guts to go to Uganda on a whim, but no guts to break up with our family. I could see Bently's soulful eyes, so disappointed in me for giving up on him. Yes, I was more worried about what the dog might think. This wasn't what I signed up for. I'd had my fill of drama watching *Newlyweds*.

Nobody who was madly in love with somebody would take off for four months to draw monkeys and Skype on Sundays. That's a no-brainer, and I knew this full well before I left. Did part of me hope that decisions would be made for me? Sure. I knew leaving my job at the spa carried a huge risk factor for future employment, but I was okay with having that door slam shut. If Cagney wanted to split up with me for going to Uganda, I would have accepted it as "fate" (fabricated fate?) and been relieved by the consequences of my actions.

Cagney's crankiness with me was understandably amplified by the African dust, cockroaches, humidity, non-running water, mosquitoes, tsetse flies, everything. When I became upset about leaving Uganda near the end of our safari, she wondered who I was having an affair with. Everyone I had ever mentioned to her in Skype chats was on the hit list. The detective was positive I was in love. No one cried that hard because they were in love with a place and were sad to leave it behind.

On Christmas Day we were poolside at the swanky Mweya Lodge. We weren't staying there, but at a crappy little hostel down the road with bunk beds and tap water the colour of mud puddles. I'd asked the front desk staff at Mweya if we could pay for a day pass at the pool and promised we'd drink a lot of beer. Cagney, who usually didn't drink, started to pound Amarula on ice and started smoking too. She hadn't smoked in twenty years, but a woman from California on our tour offered Cagney a cigarette, and she bought her own pack the very next day. I'd created a smoking monster. I knew that none of this was easy for Cagney. I'm surprised I didn't start smoking too.

A bruiser of a storm was rolling in, and we were scheduled to take a late-afternoon river cruise on the Kazinga Channel that connected two Rift Valley lakes: Edward and George (named after Queen Victoria's son and heir, Edward VII, and his own successor, George V). I busied myself with binoculars and the trumpeting elephants at the water's edge, avoiding the detective's interrogation about who I had sent emails to from the hotel's Internet café. Once our group loaded onto the boat, I climbed the ladder to the top deck for a reprieve from the accusations that were coming at me full tilt. I was "obviously" having an affair with somebody and couldn't wait to email them at every opportunity.

I zoomed my camera lens on some spindly-legged spoonbills, desperate to shake all the distractions in my head. I was finally alone with my "lover," Africa. Why was that so difficult to comprehend? Hippos bobbed along the shore, grunting pig-like before submerging and reappearing with a spray. Nile crocs slithered in and out while wading birds nonchalantly picked their way around everyone, oblivious to danger. Two fish eagles swooped lower and landed in unobstructed view (they look like bald eagles, but double the size). I focused my binoculars, listening to the excited snaps of long-lens cameras and whoops of excitement. I took a look with my naked eye and brushed arms with the woman standing beside me. "Sorry—I was so focused on the eagles! Do you want to take a look?" I asked.

I passed the binoculars to her and for the next hour, we shared them back and forth, talking birds and everything else. This would be my greatest Christmas gift—meeting Chantal Jacques. She asked me why I chose Uganda for safari and I shared my extended story, of how I came to volunteer at the Jane Goodall Institute in Entebbe. She couldn't believe it. Chantal was the co-director of a chimp sanctuary in the Congo. What were the odds? We swapped chimp stories, Bwindi gorilla trekking experiences and pivotal life moments. Her twin sister was a massage therapist in Belgium. We covered a lot of ground on that Kazinga Channel cruise and the storm held, though the bruised clouds hung low and threatening in the distance.

Cagney stayed in the cool of the lower part of the boat that had seats while Chantal and I took in the stellar views from up top.

The last place I wanted to be was sitting down below with Cagney and her cold-case investigation. I clung to Uganda like a lifeline but was losing my grip. In just a few days, we'd fly back to Canada. Then what? Cagney was prepared to end it all, so why did I keep suggesting we try to work the kinks out? I was making both of us homicidal with my lack of decision-making. I didn't want any public confrontations, and I didn't want my African safari marred by a full-on breakup. I was stalling until I had a solid exit plan.

A few days after we returned to Abbotsford in January, with the red dust of Uganda still in my shoelaces and jean stitching, Chantal emailed me. "I know you've just returned home to Canada, but would you consider volunteering here at the chimp sanctuary in the Congo? We could really use the help, especially in July."

I couldn't wait to get back.

14.

Flight Risk: The Congo

"IF YOU REALLY CARED about the chimps or Africa so much, you'd donate the money to people who have the skills to actually do something and not be so selfish," said Cagney. Cagney and I were still "together" but butting heads about the direction of our relationship. I'm surprised she didn't place me under house arrest. She was still smoking, more than ever: "And I hope you know that's completely your fault."

An emotionally smarter individual than me would have put an obviously dying relationship out of its misery for good. I felt sorry for Cagney for all the wrong reasons and couldn't end things. I was never the one to be the ender. My feeble excuses were the sort that analysts would be able to see from a hundred paces as typical of a "rescuer" identity. Cagney always referred to herself as an "orphan" because both her parents were dead. I was supposed to be her family now and the weight of this responsibility was enormous. How do you get out of family? I didn't want her to be alone again—orphaned again (as she would definitely remind me). So this was somehow better, me staying. Or rather, staying but leaving to go to the Congo.

I was going through the motions at the spa and crying my head off pretty much on a daily basis. I was already consumed by the Congo and barely operating in the real world. I listened to one song by Jann Arden like it was my intravenous. She had sent me an early clip of "All the Days" from her studio, and no song had ever shaken my insides more. It was the kind of song that I wanted as my relationship anthem (instead of Paul Simon's "50 Ways to Leave Your Lover," which was on repeat in my head).

To deep dive even further into a distressed state, I made a list of my upcoming Congolese expenses. I'll tell you right now—there are no seat sales to take advantage of. My flight alone cost $3,771.39. The Congolese visa was cheap enough ($115 US), but the staples racked up quickly: more anti-malaria drugs, a passport renewal, tampons, eucalyptus oil (for the chimps), laminated maps of Canada (Chantal's request) and maple syrup, because. Yet I had lots of theories to justify jetting off to Africa again. My daily horoscope was clearly pointing toward the Congo. My dreams were still about snakes and hummingbirds (now they were biting me): another definitive indicator. The lapse between Uganda and the Congo was somehow too long, despite the six-month span. Again, someone with a higher emotional IQ would have ended the relationship and carried on sooner, but I stayed and waited—my head, unfairly, entirely somewhere else, somewhere 13,960 kilometres away.

And then we found out that Mila, Gillian's gorgeous eleven-year-old Lab, was dying. She had cancer all through her stomach and adjacent organs. My only sadness in leaving "home" again, so soon after being in Uganda for four months, was leaving Mila. She wasn't supposed to live very long after her diagnosis—it could be sudden. The vet expected that she would lose her appetite entirely or be unable to keep food down. "She will let you know," the veterinarian told us. I couldn't stand thinking that Mila might make that decision while I was so far away. I smothered her in love before I left, telling her I'd love to see her again, but I'd understand if she couldn't wait. Bently was a nervous wreck from it all, his senses detecting something wrong with his best friend.

The morning I left for the Congo was a heartbreaker, as I looked at their sweet blurred dog faces in the frosted privacy-glass pane beside the front door. I could see them clearly, Mila's white head, Bently's big blond one crowding her out. On the telling flip side, saying goodbye to Cagney was too casual as we exchanged the kind of hug you'd awkwardly give your boss at a Christmas party—not the kind of hug you should be giving a girlfriend before getting on a plane to Africa.

But I couldn't miss this flight; I had breakfast to make for chimps in the Congo. And I had to call my parents, or I'd never hear the end of it, from a greasy pay phone at the Vancouver airport. Once again, me heading into parts unknown. My parents, once again, fretting their heads off. My mom said, "Don't be getting any ideas. I know Jane Goodall took her mom with her into the jungle and had her catching butterflies, but I'm not doing that." This was true—Dr. Leakey wouldn't allow Jane to conduct her research in Tanzania solo, so Jane's solution was grabbing her mom for the ride. My dad advised, "Don't let any of those ticks get you." There was an unspoken question in their farewells: Why couldn't I blow off steam in Vegas or on a nice sunny package holiday to Puerto Vallarta?

Oh, because I needed adventure—and that's exactly what I got when I missed my crucial flight from Nairobi to Lubumbashi, stuck in the gridlock of a mandatory transit visa line. This wasn't like a North American airport, where your name is called a dozen times if you are missing from a flight. I missed the gate by mere minutes. The next flight to the Congo wasn't for another two days. I could have flown to Addis or Johannesburg, but that would have only taken me farther from my destination to pace in a different airport.

I was grateful for my recent Ugandan experience; otherwise, thoughts of making my way about Nairobi, solo, would have set off a colossal panic attack. My bigger worry was trying to reach Chantal to let her know, as I knew the airport was some distance from her house and mobile reception was dodgy. Of course, I didn't have a cellphone with me. (I still don't.) Trying to find a phone at the Nairobi airport was a feat of all kinds. Internet was available in one corner of a store selling carvings and ground coffee, but they charged an extortion-ate rate of two US dollars a minute. There were no lockers to dump my bags (because of bomb issues in the past), so I schlepped my gear back and forth across sleeping bodies and prayer rugs in the con-gested hallways and asked an airport security officer where I might find a phone. "There's a guy who sells magazines at Gate 9. He will let you use his cellphone for four dollars a minute." Phone sex op-erators don't even charge that much! I had to pony up the money. Fortunately, I made a lucky connection with Chantal.

I'd been to Nairobi in January for one night, staying at a hotel that was also a car wash and karaoke club. Even though it was familiar, karaoke at any time is not cool—and less cool at four in the morning. I found out that I could sleep in the airport transit lounge for four hours for twenty-five dollars (US). And then along came Betty. She herded me into her tourism office of faded safari posters from the 1970s and force-fed me the idea of staying at Central Park Hotel downtown for $170 US a night. Betty insisted that I would be bored anywhere else and pushed the Central Park digs on me. And she would only accept cash. I could pay her right then and there for the room.

When I asked about cheaper options, she assured me that I would be robbed. "See your laptop—gone!" She snapped her fingers for emphasis. "Everything you own, if you stay somewhere that I do not recommend, will be gone. Then you will say, 'Betty, why you not tell me about this?' and I will say, 'I did, Jules Trotsky, I did.'" I corrected Betty on my non-Russian last name and she asked if I was racist. Because if I was not Russian, then I was probably American and most likely racist. Then she asked where I was really from, and when I said Canada, she observed, "You have all this hair on your face that I could shave. It is for the cold in Canada, I guess." Betty was obviously a charm school grad. She then went on a rant about developed countries like Canada bringing the swine flu to Africa. "But I will live longer than you, probably. My skin makes me resistant—you go pink and get rashes like the other white people, not so resistant. Like Michael Jackson, he tried to go white, and now—look—dead."

Nairobi was a pleasant enough blur, thanks in part to Betty's hotel pick. I ran on Central Park's vintage treadmill (the surrounding streets were heavily congested with goat and donkey traffic), listening to Kenny Rogers on repeat ("The Gambler"—who doesn't love to work out to that?), and then checked out Nairobi National Park (Kenya's first park), just seven kilometres south of the city. Here, you can see elephants and skyscrapers at the same time. I kissed a giraffe as all the tourists are pressed into doing. (It's like getting a wet fish slapped across your face.) Some zookeepers let me go into a cage with four young cheetahs, and my crankiness over a missed flight spun right around. But I still couldn't wait to get to the Congo.

At the airport in Lubumbashi, the president of the Congo had landed shortly after our flight had, so all passengers were locked in the airport while the red carpet was rolled out and he was shuttled away by a SWAT team of armed guards and fancy cars. The airport was a mob scene. There was no such thing as a lineup, but Chantal had a grip on me before I even saw her. She was waiting with two "protocols" who whisked me through the din of locals and armed airport officials like I was a celebrity. The men flanked me and in a fast exchange of US money, passport, visa and immunization cards, I was pushed through to the other side of Immigration. The hired men grabbed my bags and ensured that I wasn't grabbed in the chaos. With such beefed-up security and feverish chaos, I worried for a brief moment about what I had signed up for.

What did I sign up for? *Jeunes Animaux Confisqués au Katanga* (Young Animals Confiscated in Katanga), or J.A.C.K., is an independent, self-funded NGO that started in Lubumbashi in April 2006. The sanctuary for confiscated chimpanzees is run, voluntarily, by two Belgian primate lovers, Franck and Roxane Chantereau. When I arrived in July 2009, Franck and Roxane needed to return to Belgium for a month to drum up some financial support for J.A.C.K. Chantal, whose school year had ended, was going to run the show with the small crew of six dedicated staff members. And me—who had drawn chimpanzees from a safe distance in Budongo but never interacted with them.

(In Abbotsford, I had volunteered at SAINTS—Senior Animals in Need in Today's Society—a refuge for senior and special-needs animals that were abandoned: cats, dogs, llamas, horses and one pig. I spent most of my time there on my knees, cleaning up urine from aged, incontinent cats and dogs. The rooms were suffocating to me—with sadness and the stench—but bless the nurse who had the heart to provide a home for their little faces.)

Wiping up animal piss would come in handy, I learned, as Chantal and I were also in charge of babysitting Mikai, a rambunctious chimp too young to overnight at the refuge with the extreme temperature drops of winter. During the day, the Congo can reach a favourable twenty-eight degrees Celsius (eighty-two Fahrenheit), but at night, there is a plummet to fifteen teeth-chattering degrees Celsius (fifty-nine Fahrenheit). I could see my breath most mornings as we headed out just after sunrise. Mikai joined the other chimps in the "baby enclosure" during the day, quickly losing her diaper and tiny T-shirt to become a member of the wild again. She could climb as high as the others, and she often walked in tandem with her pal, a chimp called Santa, on the ground. Santa and her pot-belly became my favourite in no time. She had been the "lucky star" of the Congolese military, bringing them good luck and protection in battle in Kivu. Santa would be carried at the front of the line as they went into combat. Imagine the terror that she witnessed.

Learning the names of my charges was the first mission. Dian was easy—she was the crybaby of the lot, sticking to her best chum Africa and wailing inconsolably if they were separated. If Dian didn't get her bottle fast enough, or a banana was stolen from her hands, she was crying again, much like my kid sister. Pasa was easily picked out of the crowd too. As soon as he was within tickling reach, he'd flop on his back, squirming, desperate for a good tickle. He would laugh like a maniac and pull all his limbs into a tight ball—and then beg for more.

Coco had belonged to the Congolese president's family. When he learned that keeping a chimp was illegal, he brought Coco to J.A.C.K. (with a camera crew in tow). Wanza arrived at the refuge as an alcoholic who refused to accept milk for the first six months. Timid Kala was owned by a Chinese copper mine bigwig who had carted her around to bars as a circus act. She had a deeply scarred, hairless patch on her right shoulder where cigarettes were butted out on her skin. Tongo, the smallest and youngest of the adult group, was constantly being pulled between Seki and Mwisho. They fought over her, wanting to take care of the youngster. Mwisho, who didn't like bread at all, actually collected bread for Tongo and kept it protected in his arms while the others prowled like henchmen for pieces to steal from the younger ones.

Cheetah and Seki, who arrived at the refuge together, were attached at the hairy hip and walked as though they were wearing a horse costume. Cheetah was the head and Seki pulled up the rear. Two years before my arrival, there had been a tragic fire in the night enclosure when an arsonist set fire to the dry hay in the cage. Two of the chimps had died—one of smoke inhalation, the other of severe burns to her entire body. When bush fires burned in Lubumbashi, Cheetah and Seki became extremely anxious. The smell of smoke terrified them, a painful reminder of the night they escaped and two of their family members perished. Other chimps at J.A.C.K. had been caught and injured in wire snare traps set by black-market traders. The traps are set on the ground, and because chimps walk on their knuckles, they easily step into the hidden wire loops and become dangerously and sometimes fatally entangled.

My first few days at the zoo, learning the stories of each chimp's arrival at the refuge, were emotionally exhausting. But hope was the powerful antidote—coupled with Mikai's antics. I had never put a diaper on a human baby before, let alone a chimp with four legs to contend with. Mikai caught on to my inexperienced hands immediately and turned each morning into a chase scene. I could often get one adhesive strip pasted down—but it would be on her hair, not on the other bit of the diaper. Mikai would have it ripped off in a few strides and would resume bonking the poor kitten at Franck's house over the head with an empty coffee mug. That cat must have had a cement head, because the clunks were not unlike those of a coconut being split.

My days were hectic and full of responsibility. (Ahem.) I shook my head so many times in the first few days that I must have looked like one of those bobble-head dolls that you mount on a car dash. There would be zero chance of me having an experience like this in Canada. I'd need a PhD or zoology degree or some serious credentials to even be considered for a job or volunteer position at a zoo or sanctuary. If you're willing to volunteer (and pay to get yourself there), sanctuaries like J.A.C.K. overlook the credentials in favour of passion and support. It was the single best decision I had ever made, despite all the flak from certain parties, the dent in my bank account and the upheaval at the spa. It didn't matter—all of it, all of the Congo, was phenomenal. There is no greater feeling than holding a warm chimp in your arms.

I had never in my life woken up so early for so many consecutive days. Alarms went off at 4:30 to 4:45 a.m. Chantal would turn the stove elements on (provided there was electricity) to get the pots of water warming. It took an hour to bring a pot to a boil. We'd have juice and slices of bread with pâté or soft cheese in the dim light of the kitchen while Mikai slept. She'd be up soon enough, hopefully after we'd downed a cup of coffee and prepped all the bottles of milk for the chimps at the sanctuary.

Dozens of one-litre plastic bottles dominated the space beside the sink in the crowded prep kitchen. The six youngest chimps had their own personal bottles with pacifier tops. Chronically bleary-eyed until noon, I stationed myself at the stove with Chantal, carefully measuring honey, propolis, vitamins and powdered milk into a narrow funnel. Any chimp with a respiratory issue would get a few drops of eucalyptus oil.

This was serious business. Chimps are as particular as we are; if the milk was too hot or too cold, they pushed it away in disgust. Not enough honey or too much propolis and they balked. Tall, full fat, no whip, extra honey or else! The adults accepted the warm milk poured into tin cups with handles in a semi-mannerly way, unless they decided to toss it back on you for a laugh. The shrill feeding-time pant-hoots and excited displays from the adult chimps were deafening.

Mikai had her bottle with a little strawberry yogurt and whatever fruit she would steal from the pantry. Waking her up was a sweet experience. She slept nestled in blankets in a small dog cage. We covered the cage with a blanket too (like my grandmother did for her budgies). Once Chantal and I had ourselves gathered (because all hell would break loose once Mikai was up and on a tear), one of us would nudge Mikai awake. Sometimes she'd already have her eyes open, blinking brightly and innocently at me. Other times, she was still deep in slumber, in her little T-shirt to keep warm.

"Mikai...time to get up." Although I haven't had a lot of baby experience, I imagine this is what it's like: the arms that reach out for you and cuddle in for safety, the big yawns and burps and the gentle morning hellos and love. And then the games began. Mikai liked to rip her diaper off, if you didn't get to it fast enough, and she'd fly into the kitchen to get at something—bottles of vegetable oil (to pour over her head, naturally), cans of Coca-Cola, a handful of sugar, a delicious bar of soap. My Nikes were another go-to for play. She'd grab the laces and swing them around like a lasso. Again, at the cat's head, wrecking ball–style. For someone only knee-high, she was a destructive force. (I assume all mothers are nodding along here.)

After our assembly line of breakfast bottle production ended, Chantal and I would have the house guard load up the truck. Chantal had to stop me a few times from grabbing boxes, reminding me that I was taking the job away from someone else. "There's somebody to do that for us." I felt quite useless a lot of the time in the Congo. There was someone to do the laundry, wash dishes, mop the floors, load the truck, open the house gate, pack the groceries off the conveyor belt, bring groceries to the car, feed the cat, help you parallel park, wash the car—it was surreal. "If you do any of these things, somebody is out of a job," I was told.

After we had completed our breakfast run at the zoo and checked the electric fence for connectivity (before the adult chimps were released into the outdoor enclosures), there was time to observe the adults and babes at play. There were always errands to run, for papayas or day-old bread from the bakery, before the next hot-milk feeding at around five in the afternoon—the staff would provide fruit, cabbage and eggs throughout the day.

Chantal had bought me a membership at the Lubumbashi Golf Course. "It's the only safe place for you to run here," she warned me. Though I was accustomed to running later in the day, I took my runs when I could, and they were often after feeding the chimps breakfast and prior to errands. I'd do a few laps, high-stepping certain snake-friendly areas, and snicker to see the golf course staff stretched out on the back nine, sleeping in the shade. There were rarely golfers here (a few mining executives or UN workers). Chantal and I were the most consistent, non-golfing, visitors. I couldn't help but think of Kim when I ran around the course. She'd get a big kick out of the sleeping staff and the homemade signs warning guests about "flying balls." She was an amazing golfer. Kim would have loved the morning beer routine too.

Chantal and I would land at the golf course around 8:30 a.m. She'd find a chair in the sun and read while I lapped the course and returned, soggy with sweat, half an hour later. Like clock-work, Chantal would say, "It's time to take your beer." At nine in the morning! We'd been up since 4:30, so technically it was noon in our world. Chantal didn't drink, but she knew I had an affection for good beer (especially the Belgian brews of her homeland). At the golf course, I could choose between a bottle of Simba (Lion) or Tembo (Elephant). The bottles were traditional African size: 750 millilitres. Congolese beer had hand-painted labels, though; if you held one in your hand long enough, the white paint would lift and smear.

As I was having my usual morning post-run beer (which became a fast tradition), Chantal had her traditional Coke and smoke and asked our server for some potato chips. She told me about the "canaries" (yellow-suited police officers) and the random "toll booths," where the suggested payment is 500 to 1,500 francs. The officers earn about $130 US a month but pad their wallets with these friendly stops. Oddly, there are no coins in the Congo and only three bank notes (100, 200 and 500 francs). Your wallet can easily be as thick as a New York sirloin but contain only ten bucks (500 francs equals one US dollar). In town, yawning men in cowboy hats and rubber boots sit with stacks of cold, hard francs, ready to exchange for US dollars. This is completely acceptable, and it is recommended, versus a bank exchange with a pocket-gouging rate of return.

Fascinated as I was by this information, I had to interrupt Chantal. "These chips taste like soap." She laughed. "It's cheap shipping. They deflate the chip bags to make more room in the boxes and pack them in trucks with detergent. So sometimes the chips taste like soap."

There were numerous and enormous differences between Uganda and the Congo. The Congolese response to *mizungos* (white people) is what surprised me the most. In Entebbe, kids mobbed me like I was a red-carpet star, yelling "America!" "Obama!"

"*Mizungo*! What is your name?" and more commonly, "*Mizungo*, give me money!" In Lubumbashi there was the occasional stare, but the (white) Belgian presence over the years created an obvious difference of awareness and acceptance. The copper mines in Lubumbashi are largely Asian owned, and there is a sizable Greek and Lebanese population as well, making the Congo more multicultural than Abbotsford, BC.

One night, when I was poking through the local market with Cyril, a (white) French student, a vendor greeted us: "Hello, Mr. and Mrs. White. Come, buy something." Due to protests from other Messrs. and Mrs. White, who were irritated with the frequent stops imposed by police asking for documents and visas, the governor implemented a "Courtesy Month," scheduled to take place every July. For this month, no arrests can be made, and officers are not allowed to ask for any documents.

The road that passes by the president's summer house is dotted with canaries and AK-47-armed security, and it comes with its own unique regulations. When the president is in Lubumbashi, the road to his house (which is a major thoroughfare) is closed, and the ever-present gangs of street kids are taken about fifty kilometres out of the city for the duration of his stay. You can't overtake another car on the road in front of the president's house. The speed limit is forty kilometres per hour, and there is absolutely no honking permitted. (Try to tell that to the one-year-old chimp riding shotgun! Mikai loved to lean on the horn.)

"I could never live in Belgium again," Chantal told me one day, exhaling a plume of smoke. "Too many rules." I nearly spat out my soapy chips and a few bubbles. The Congo, to me, was full of unspoken rules. If you park your car, odds are that when you return, it will have been washed by entrepreneurial street kids hoping for five hundred francs or so. Chantal told me that in Zambia, the same creative money-making spirit is witnessed along the highways, where young men will fill potholes to improve the roads—then stop drivers and demand money to compensate for their selfless road-improvement work.

The billboards along the main roads advertised all the essentials for Lubumbashi life: cooking oil, Nokia cellphones (there are no land lines here) and skin-lightening lotions (in this colonized country, lighter skin means power and wealth). This was life in cosmopolitan Lubumbashi, a city of four million with one fax machine, a zoo, one vet and a Greek restaurant with a basketball court that served very tasty garlicky goat testicles and crispy frog legs. And thin-crust pizzas loaded with ham and, surprise, bananas!

Chantal and I would linger at the zoo to see the bush babies emerge in the evenings with their big, blinking eyes, the size of golf balls. At sundown, we'd return to the sanctuary with all the fixings for a chimp dinner. It was an ever-changing menu, depending on donations—grapes, hard-boiled eggs, mango, buns, lettuce, pumpkin, sweet potatoes, cassava (manioc). After dinner, one of the J.A.C.K. guards would close the gate behind us as the chimps began to bed down. The "nesting" began immediately after eating as each found its own spot and fashioned a makeshift nest out of straw.

Mikai did not observe such calculated patterns. She was like a kid high on a Halloween candy binge. We'd pile back in the Land Rover with her hanging off the handles above the windows, swinging in her diaper-butt. Chantal would pull over in our sundowner spot where we'd watch the giant Congo sun slip into the earth. I realize it's the same sun we have in Canada, but for some reason, it appeared a hundred times bigger. Always a fire orange. Always amazing.

Chantal and I had been full tilt with the sanctuary and a 24-7 commitment, save for one day when she took me to a secret quarry for a picnic. "Working" every day at the sanctuary was the most enlightening thing I'd ever done. In between admiring the chimps and making breakfast shakes for the gang, Chantal made sure that I saw and felt every inch of her beloved Congo. She insisted I experience her friend Antoine's frog legs—his were the very best. I tried every Belgian beer I could find at the grocer's and ordered a "cheese and human egg sandwich" at a deli just to see what it was. The next time we went to that same deli, I had the "pancakes with comedy," as the lost-in-translation menu advertised. Turns out that "comedy" was (a misspelling of?) ice cream. I never did figure out what the "human egg" was.

Everyone spoke French in Lubumbashi. Except me. Although I'd taken years of imposed French classes in school, I still sounded like a dumb five-year-old, managing not much more than: "I'm hot," "I'm cold," or "I'm hungry." Chantal was fluent in several languages. She treated me to the finest things (*merci!*), and of all the places I've travelled, the food in the Congo is still the unparalleled standout. We had Lebanese shawarma, delicate French pastries, knockout pizzas, fragrant eggplant curries, spiced sausages on the grill, farmer's pâté (that I still crave) and wheels and wheels of fine cheese.

But the Congo was not all about brie and tickling chimps. I was well aware of the dangers of the storied dark Congo. It's synonymous with Ebola outbreaks and civil wars. I heard reports of countless Congolese women who were raped by the militia and army in the north. Chantal told me within minutes of my arrival in Lubumbashi, "You are not gay here." She knew I was openly gay in Canada, but this was not to be discussed in the Congo, ever. When you are in a host country, you learn to respect local customs, or you go to jail. Same-sex activity has always been legal in the Congo, but there is no legal protection against discrimination. There is no recognition of same-sex unions or same-sex adoption rights, let alone protection from hate speech, violence or discrimination in the workplace. Although I was avidly gay and rainbow-flag-waving proud back in Canada, the reality and risks trumped any notion I might have had about being oblivious to the cultural stigmas in the Congo. My hotheaded younger self may have rebelled (as suggested during my unsuccessful Canada World Youth interview nearly fifteen years before) and dismissed Chantal's cautionary words, but I wasn't a fool. This was Chantal's country, quirks and all. She shrugged her shoulders and said, frankly, that if you wanted to have somebody killed, homosexual or not, this could be done in exchange for twelve beers. They don't even have to be cold; street kids will happily do anything for beer.

The ugly scars of two civil wars (1996 to 1997 and 1998 to 2003) were most pronounced in a widespread famine that saw the decimation and extinction of many wild animal species. Half the gorilla population in Kahuzi-Biega National Park, for example, was killed for bush meat during those conflicts. Displaced Congolese moved into the forests to escape violence and became involved in the exotic pet trade and poaching activity. Elephants at the zoo were slaughtered by locals as a food source, and the wild rhinos, giraffes, hyenas, okapis, zebras, warthogs and buffaloes were wiped out completely. Gone forever.

Chantal had been born in the Congo, and her serene childhood memories included slithering snakes, fluttering butterflies (now seemingly obsolete), abundant birds and the heady scent of coffee plantations. Now the coffee is imported from Kenya, and eerily, few birds sing. The once booming copper mines are feeling the extended reach of the recession that slammed America in 2008. The once thriving coffee industry was another casualty of the ongoing violence and political crises. Armed militia and government soldiers overtook land, and coffee farms were simply abandoned during the war years.

Chantal also told me about the militia-imposed curfews of her childhood and how she watched an elementary school classmate at the Ecole Belge be killed in front of her by a soldier because she'd opened the gate to the school after the 4:00 p.m. curfew. Chantal and her twin sister were thrown in jail for a day for not producing official identification at age ten. She shared vivid memories of the militia invading her home and firing rounds of bullets into the ceiling to ensure that her family wasn't hiding any mercenaries. Her father was jailed on a regular basis, and this was normal.

At La Brioche, the bakery we frequented, half a dozen amputees routinely leaned against the bakery wall with makeshift crutches, some parked in primitive hand-pedal-powered wheelchairs. I asked Chantal if they were victims of land-mine explosions or the civil war. "They probably had a minor injury or an infection, couldn't afford the health care [as one has to buy everything during a hospital visit: food, sheets, medications], so developed gangrene and lost their leg."

There are no traffic rules, stoplights work only occasionally, and there are few mere fender-benders in Lubumbashi. When there is an accident, everyone dies, and the number of deaths can be shocking. The *fula fulas* (minivan taxis) often carry more than thirty people at a time. A few weeks before I arrived, a *fula fula* overtook Chantal on the road and collided head-on with a truck— and thirty-five people died. After such accidents, Chantal told me, there can be mob scenes, as friends of crash victims will kill in revenge. Hearses transporting coffins in ornate glass aquarium-like cases while broadcasting instrumental songs passed by us almost daily.

Every day in the Congo was precious and perplexing. It was daunting and rewarding—but the dangers never left my peripheral vision. I could feel my brain's cortex overheating with all the sensory information it had to process at every turn. I felt on fire, ready...for what, I wasn't quite sure. I was quick to shut down any thoughts of Canada and all that was connected to returning. There would be time enough to stew about that on the eighteen-hour flight home.

I didn't Skype Cagney the cop from the Congo. We had agreed that these stilted and buffered conversations led to too many battles. Emails were exchanged at a normal pace, but without the longing and "miss you" that should have been there. Mostly we talked about Mila's status. And yet, I was having the time of my life. My month in Lubumbashi was going by too fast. Each morning when I'd pop a Malarone (anti-malaria pill) out of its foil packet, I could visibly see how many precious days I had left.

I wasn't in any big rush to leave my endorphin-laced existence in the Congo, and Cagney didn't have to be a genuine detective to detect that. I was a barely recognizable version of myself. I didn't mind waking at 4:30 a.m. to make breakfast for a resilient group of chimps that had endured so much. I didn't care that I was sleeping in Franck and Roxane's ten-year-old son's lumpy single bed. It was all part of the beautiful package. There was such nourishment in my days. It was a routine of perfect design, right down to the post-run detergent-flavoured chips and beer for brunch. I liked being detached from a lot of things, maybe—like Cagney, responsibility and massage therapy.

However, I also liked being attached. I felt stitched to a cause and something outside of myself, at least temporarily. I was floored at the commitment and funding that operating a chimp sanctuary took. Franck and Roxane had handed their lives over to the chimps, while I was merely stopping in for a month for a glossy version of Congolese vacation. Making breakfast for twenty-three chimps with Chantal in the Congo had worked the perfect alchemy for me, offering stimulation and complete wonder on a daily basis.

But the month was over. I'd be flying back to Canada in the morning.

15.

On a Yacht in Amsterdam

"Why don't you just go home?"

For once, I didn't protest. Rain pelted down (as it seemed to do every day in Abbotsford). I had probably been bitching about that very rain and everything else that was making me miserable. I played tug-of-war with a disinterested Mila. She hadn't died while I was away but seemed to be drifting closer in that direction. I could not hold on to happiness in BC. I did all the things that were recommended by fortune cookies, my daily horoscope, Oprah and like-minded influencers. After Uganda, I signed up for a falconry course. I bought some blank canvases and turned my attention to painting a few commissions. I trained for a half-marathon, wrote a book in forty days, took workshops on illustrating books, painted storefront windows for the holidays and once again cleaned up piss at the rescue centre for senior animals. But after being in the Congo, my happiness bar had been raised to a nearly unattainable point.

It was as if Cagney was speaking Russian and I was replying in Khoisan click dialect. We had lost our lingua franca. She thought that letting me sleep in and read the newspaper over coffee was love. I thought this was a given. She washed and shined my Suzuki Sidekick as a form of love—but it wasn't something that I really cared about. In turn, I sent her long, hilarious emails throughout the day, which were responded to with brevity. I wanted more than an acronym and an emoticon. I received haikus and LOLs. We were speaking different love languages. *No comprende*. I didn't want the routine that I was trapped in—one that Cagney would say was part of being an adult and responsible. Time and time again I heard: "You can't have fun in life all the time. You have to do things you don't like."

I stopped citing sources that disputed this and moved into the guest bedroom across from the bedroom I once shared with Cagney. It was a guest bedroom with no bed. I borrowed a mattress from Gillian, and despite the oppressive tension just outside the door of this room, I felt like I could breathe for once. I could sleep in, stare, read, Facebook—all without a timekeeper. I started looking for apartments and jobs in Toronto in the privacy of my guest room. I quit my spa job for the final time, with apologies to my very patient boss. After so many brutal hours of commuting to classes to attain my registration in the province, I resigned from the BC College of Massage Therapists with a promise that I wouldn't be back. The secretary suggested I go inactive, in case I had a change of heart—this would be an easier process than resigning from the college. I assured her that I was totally okay with this risk—I wanted to resign from the whole province, in general. In between looking for apartments in Cabbagetown, I placed an ad on Craigslist for my Sidekick and sold it for two thousand dollars a week later.

I spent as much time as I could by Mila's side. There were no rules at this point—if Mila wanted a cupcake, so be it. She ate more off my plate than I did most days. Her stomach was a runway of staples from the surgery, and she seemed unable to shake the lethargy that came after the operation. Her vitality was gone, even though Gillian prepared elaborate cancer-fighting buffets with vitamin C powder, cottage cheese, yogurt with acidophilus, pumpkin, chicken, rice, eggs and liver pâté.

I moved back to Toronto two weeks after returning from the Congo, and Gillian had Mila put down a week after. It's a decision that never feels right. It's always riddled with self-doubt. Mila was supposed to tell us when it was time, not the other way around. Or maybe she had told us, and none of us wanted to believe it or face the days that would follow without her. Agnes Sligh Turnbull said it best: "Dogs' lives are too short. Their only fault, really."

I was foggy from insomnia and heartbreak for Mila. Everything was suspended again. I was sleeping on my kid brother's couch and trying to find both a job and an apartment at the same time. The timing couldn't have been worse, as the city was undergoing an influx of college and university students heading back to school. I could not find an apartment. Any leads were snapped up before I could even view them. There were bidding wars—on apartments! Dax said to take my time; it was no big deal to be on his couch. His boyfriend thought otherwise.

I ran my former route through Cabbagetown and Riverdale, picking up the path like I'd never left it. I knew all the smells: the deep fryers of Koreatown, the punch of fresh fish and ripe bananas in the open market, the wet punk of the Don River, the late-night vomit and dog piss being hosed off by shop owners on Parliament. I could hear those smells. I turned down every leafy street in Cabbagetown, on high alert for signs that said For Rent, and I found one on Winchester that I'd swing back to after a shower. I grabbed some jerk chicken at Mr. Jerk and made my way back over to the storybook two-storey brick house. There was no price and no details on the sign, but I knew I wanted a house, not a high-rise or a brownstone again.

The door was open and serious construction was going on. "Hello?"

Gord hollered back and Mike came to the door. The two brothers were installing kitchen cabinets, and drywall dust and saws were helter-skelter. But the place was a stunner—and huge.

"How much are you asking for rent?"

"It's $2,200. That includes Wi-Fi."

I must have looked shocked.

"It's a two-bedroom—is that what you're looking for?"

It wasn't. I did *not* want a roommate.

"Just so you know, it won't be ready until October first, either."

I'd already logged a few weeks on Dax's couch; what was the difference if I tacked on a few more?

I took a look around and was charmed by the architecture and possibility. The hardwood floors, moulding, tall baseboards and old fireplace—it was just the kind of place I wanted to call home. The kitchen was brand new, with granite countertops and stainless-steel everything. There were shiny new Samsung stackables and a cute backyard with a deck and towering trees. It was ideal in every way, except for that niggling two-bedroom issue. I took down Gord's number and said I'd have to really think about it. And find someone to live with me.

As I walked back to Church Street, I heard a dog whistle that could have come from only a few people in my life—my dad, Kim, Kim's sister or my ex, Kelly. (Or some construction guy in Abbotsford alerting me to a sidewalk of just-poured cement.)

It was Kelly. She was going to a hair appointment—what was I doing? I gave her a condensed version. It was serendipity that we had crossed paths again. I told her to check out the house rental the next day. I upsold the backyard, dishwasher and fancy Samsung laundry machines. Brand-new kitchen! Granite countertops! Isn't it a rite of passage? Isn't there an unspoken lesbian initiation that you have to live with an ex-girlfriend (once or twice removed) at least once? Besides, Kelly was my only viable roomie option—she was fastidious in the cleaning department and made a really great rapini, chickpea and prosciutto dish that I missed.

But after seemingly convincing her on a spontaneous move, I didn't hear from her for three days. I asked Dax if he knew of anyone looking for an apartment.

"Yeah. Me."

"What?"

John and Dax had decided to break up. But Dax couldn't live in a house; his beloved saltwater fish tank is the size of a soaker tub and required cement floors—not century-old wood floors like the Winchester house.

I knew this rental would fly off the market. I'd looked at a dozen crappy places and was less than thrilled with those options. And then Kelly finally called. "Let's go see it."

Kelly had walked past a few times and had to digest the idea of moving from an apartment that she'd lived in for nine years. It was a big deal. But she too fell for all the things I had, including the walk-in closet and mud room. There was so much space! If you've never lived in a four-hundred-square-foot apartment, you might not understand the visual adjustment to enormity—a place where your eyes can move freely about a room without a wall in the way. She was going to think about it, and again, the days lapsed and I half-heartedly looked at other options, convincing myself that

Kelly would stay in what she knew to be tried-and-true and much cheaper. Then she called. "Let's do it."

I couldn't believe it. Yes, another full-circle moment, proving my Spirograph life wound in tight circles of people and places.

My bank account was definitely skinnier after Uganda and the Congo, back to back, but I still had a cushion. I'd found three jobs, too—one of them back at the Royal York Hotel, picking up where I'd left off just years before. Half of the client list was still the same, and aside from some new gym equipment in the health club, it was like I'd never left. I landed a job at a nearby wellness centre (with a team of chiropractors, naturopaths, physiotherapists, kinesiologists and even a sleep specialist) and at Body Blitz, a women-only spa in the trendy King West neighbourhood. With a Dead Sea salt pool, a hot Epsom tub, an infrared sauna, a eucalyptus-infused steam room and a heart-stopper cold plunge pool, work became pleasure. Every shift ended with a soak and a tall vitamin D shake loaded with bananas, cocoa and honey (a meal fit for a chimp).

I frequented the Looking Glass, the only dyke bar that was left on Church Street, on weekends, and I caught some comedy acts on Bloor West—but nobody caught my eye. I was okay with that. I was still inhaling relief like someone hyperventilating into a brown paper bag. I felt reserved for the first time and less anxious to be consumed by someone (as I was prone to do). I didn't want to sacrifice my footloose lifestyle or downtown address.

In January, Kim's sister Lynne sent me an email somewhat out of the blue. Lynne knew that I had moved back to Toronto and thought it was time we all got together again. It would be the first time I had seen Kim in five or six years—and she'd be bringing her girlfriend. I'd known Kim's sister longer than I'd known Kim, and our friendship had allowed me to keep loose tabs on Kim.

I therefore already knew about Kim's girlfriend. They'd started dating four months after Kim and I had split up.

I fretted until the day of the reunion. Kim and Lynne arrived together, and then the girlfriend, a little later, with some baklava from a bakery. As I expected, Kim was as flawless and gorgeous as ever. She was neatly pressed, tanned as a coffee bean, lip-glossed, hair perfect—and I was trance-like lost in her latest fragrance. Gucci.

I served a spicy shrimp appetizer (too bad Kim's girlfriend didn't like shrimp) and we sat around the kitchen island, catching up, filling in the blanks, as I sweated profusely and fidgeted. I had rushed out that very week to buy two more bar stools to facilitate this great, unexpected reunion—something I would only do for Kim. Anyone else would have had to pull up a cross-legged seat on the floor, and I wouldn't have flinched. The big update was nothing new—Kim and her partner shared a house in Oakville and had a cat. A cat! Kim was so allergic to cats that I knew it had to be true love for her to allow this. My heart sank a little.

In March we all got together again at Café Diplomatico in Little Italy. Kim encouraged me to bring my "girlfriend" of two weeks. I had just begun seeing a comedian (yes, a comedian in real life). Kim drove me home while her girlfriend drove my girlfriend to a theatre workshop in the west end. I'm not sure how that arrangement happened, but I was more than happy with the split. Seated beside Kim in her BMW, it was like no time had lapsed. I had to remind myself that we weren't together, though it seemed so familiar. Was I reading more into Kim's long looks and wide smile?

"Kim's still in love with you, and you're in love with her," the comedian insisted later that night when she showed up on my doorstep after her workshop. Where did she get this from? Over a shared pizza at Café Dip in the span of maybe an hour? I was pretty phony at denying it. I knew I loved Kim; there was no question—that love had never stopped. But how could this two-week girlfriend see it over pizza *blanco* and Moretti? Whether this love was reciprocated from the other side of the table was unlikely. Kim had a cat now!

As much as I wanted to fall back into Kim's arms, I knew I was lost in a land of unicorns. The comedian and I had a minor blowout, and she stormed out. (I was happy to hear that something positive did come out of our brief relationship—she quickly worked me into her routine, and apparently the audience loved it. I was okay with her having the last laugh.)

Meanwhile, I diverted my energies into something concrete—writing. I signed up for an online travel-writing course to keep my brain circuits sparking. This fix was encouraging, but it made me want to travel again, in a desperate way. I'm not sure what I Googled that night in May while enjoying a free-flow pour of Merlot, but I found myself filling out an elaborate application form for a volunteer position in Maui at the Pacific Primate Sanctuary. I could live income-neutral in a yurt and pick my own fruit and veg for lunch. And hang out with monkeys all day. And then I applied to volunteer at the Drill Ranch in Nigeria (where they look after mandrills, the largest of all monkeys, who live exclusively in Africa). I wasn't picky about what kind of monkey: capuchin, white-eared marmoset, cotton-top tamarin, black-handed spider monkey…

The Pacific Primate Sanctuary responded first, and I easily shifted my gaze from Nigeria to Maui. Foraging for macadamia nuts, surfing and maybe buying a beat-up Jeep to bomb around in on weekends. I sent more details about my background and recent experience with the Jane Goodall Institute. Maybe I could illustrate a colouring book for them too? The cotton-top tamarin monkey would make for fun doodling! There were a few Skype interviews back and forth with the sanctuary founder and one of the primary animal caregivers. I was sold on the whole awesome idea. I loved Toronto, yes, but I was at a stalemate, even with three jobs on the go. Kelly was ready to move on and in with her boyfriend outside the city anyway. He had a big house in suburbia and a dog named Harley; they could put in a swimming pool if Kelly wanted. She supported my Maui idea. "Why not? There's nothing keeping you here."

There wasn't. I was a free-range chicken, save for some recent investments in Ikea bookshelves and a dresser. I felt like I was idling again, and my Kim crush wasn't exactly sustainable. I made a quick commitment to Maui without informing a lot of the necessary people involved (three bosses, two landlords). As I made the Skype call to Maui, fireworks shot off in the distance (really)—gunpowder blasts echoed off the high-rises in St. James Town. It was May 24, the Victoria Day holiday—so the fireworks weren't just in my head.

Dax had moved into a ten-storey apartment a block away. We had planned on taking the streetcar to the Beaches to see the fireworks display at Ashbridge's Bay. But Dax had a sore throat from the lethal fumes in his place: the parquet floors had been urethaned the day before. His movers weren't booked until the following weekend, so Dax was sleeping on the floor in a furnitureless apartment that looked north over the woods of Rosedale. We drank champagne out of the only two coffee mugs he had, on a duvet in the kitchen, on the floor. Dax seemed to think Maui was a good idea too. The common response seemed to be, "Why not?"

I had learned this: I was not climbing any sort of corporate ladder. Money wasn't a big lure for me—because all the really cool things required volunteering. For free. Like me, free to a good home.

I walked back to Winchester late that night, a nice champagne buzz in my head. Kelly was up, making her famous rapini, chickpea and prosciutto dish.

"Kim called. Like three times."

"Kim?"

"Yeah, sounds like she really wanted to talk."

I knew she was still working day shifts at the steel mill and would be getting up at 4:30 in the morning. I didn't want to be the one to wake her near midnight.

I called Kim the following morning (she wasn't working), apologetic that I didn't get back to her the night before. I kindly asked how her girlfriend was doing, as one should.

"We broke up."

"What?" I was floored. *So* floored that I actually, self-confidently, blurted out this: "But I just said yes to Maui!"

What this meant in my squirrelly head was—Kim was single and I had agreed to fly off to Maui and hang out with monkeys for an entire year. And Kim was single. I can't remember her exact reaction to that statement, but she likes to remind me of it. It was obvious: we were meant to be together again, and that time was now. How could I go to Maui?

Over the course of two virtual cups of coffee (mine in Toronto, hers in Oakville with the cat), all the details were laid out.

Kim was single.

Cue up Jann Arden's "Thing for You."

"So, here's something for you to think about," Kim said. "Lynne is turning fifty and bought this week on a yacht at an auction as a birthday present to herself. I was supposed to go with you-know-who, but that would be really awkward now. It will be just the captain, Lynne, Al (Lynne's husband) and me. Do you want to come to Amsterdam for a week with us?"

A week on a yacht around the fabled canals of Holland with Kim? Who was now single? Yes! Of course I wanted to go. I found myself looking at flight deals to Amsterdam and booked one that night. I knew what I wanted. Kim had ruined me for anyone else. Did she feel the same? She was just days post-break up, and I already had her pinned down as my girlfriend.

Kelly shrugged her shoulders when I shared the news about jetting off to Holland. "Well, you never stopped being in love with her, did you?"

Kim and I talked for the entire overnight flight (seven hours). Amsterdam was like our honeymoon spot. We slid easily into a very comfortable space with each other, like no years had separated us. We had so much ground to cover, and I ate up all the details I'd missed from her life. Golf scores, hockey tournaments, trips, the cat, stuff that she'd been building in her workshop—all of it. By the time we took the train to meet our captain, we were flatlining on energy. Captain Ken gave us a warm welcome with sweet cinnamon-laced *appeltaart* and tumblers of advocaat, a thick Dutch take on eggnog that tastes more like boozy custard.

We immediately began our day on the water and gently motored off to our first marina in the direction of Gouda. We moved on from advocaat, and Ken passed around the iconic green bottled Grolsch and pickled herring. By the time we docked, the June twilight was dreamy. The moon had a full belly and hung just above the wooden windmills in a cantaloupe sky. Kim gave me a look that I recognized from long ago.

We would be sharing the front berth of the yacht together— a space that was best described by Kim as a "Trivial Pursuit pie piece." It was semi-claustrophobic and not exactly soundproof. We lay back in our Trivial Pursuit triangle, buzzing from the time difference, beers in the sun and all that was unfolding.

It was happening.

16.
Caretakers of History

I CANCELLED MY YEAR-IN-A-YURT plans in Maui in a heart-beat. It was clear that Kim was a sure thing.

And so, a year and a half later, on the snowiest, blowiest day of January, Kim and I were in a moving truck trundling down a construction-clogged Spadina Avenue in Toronto, the door finally closed on our former addresses. We were ready to be under one roof instead of shuttling back and forth, packing bags, laundering, rinse, lather, repeat, to and fro. We had been looking for a few months, taking advantage of shared days off, to see as many houses as we could.

Kim and I were about to give up, but on the day before Halloween we slated a last-ditch effort: we'd view four more houses with a seasoned realtor and push our boundary out to Cambridge, about an hour from downtown Toronto. Galt was its own inde-pendent city prior to an amalgamation with Hespeler, Preston and Blair as "Cambridge" in 1973. Most of Galt's population resisted the abrupt marriage. Though it was officially part of Cambridge,

Galt's name proved it had staying power. West Galt would be a forty-five-minute commute to the steel mill where Kim worked. Her twelve-hour shifts were compounded by extra driving time, so the radius had to be fair to her first and foremost. We chose the neighbourhood because it was a reasonable drive for Kim; it was a temporary, work-related, geographical decision for both of us. Kim had worked with the same company for nearly thirty years, so changing jobs wasn't an option. I wouldn't be able to get to my Toronto massage jobs without a car and a traffic meltdown, but I was confident I could pick up something local in a snap.

Cambridge wasn't our desired area, but we were grasping at real-estate straws. The first three houses we looked at had been sitting on the market for a reason (dumpy neighbours, a bow in an exterior wall, questionable structural issues and a punky basement). We were less than enthused about looking at the last house—it was the least promising of them all, from the grainy pictures online. But in person, the 1861 granite and limestone cottage, the last house we were to view, was a stunner.

Kim had never lived in a "used" house, as her ex called them; she had lived only in brand-new builds in suburbia. I *wanted* used. I wanted charm and personality and history and heritage. I had none of the skills required to maintain such a property, but Kim did. As soon as we stepped inside, I had our furniture instantly arranged. Kim remarked on the potent wet-dog smell, but I was hanging art on the walls—the twelve-inch stone walls would still be standing even after an apocalypse. The pine and hickory floors told their own story. A line on the wall to the basement showed a former stair stringer that ran up to the attic, where the children would have slept in the early 1900s.

It was the cutesy carriage house attached to the kitchen, with the original threshing boards, that sold me in a nanosecond.

The exposed stone walls and surprise Murphy bed made for a really sweet guest space. The kitchen was bright (sombrero yellow!) and had neat design elements, like the leather-wrapped granite countertops and apron sink. The deck just off the kitchen was stone— and on top of that stone was a giant Fred Flintstone-esque stone table (which would require a crane to move).

Admittedly, I was the one with the bigger crush on the stone cottage, with its pine-shake roof and corkscrew hazel in the front. Two black walnut trees towered in the back, and after being in cement-stacked Toronto for so many years, I was thrilled with all the green. (Not so thrilled with the ten thousand walnuts that fell that fall, but they were part of the package.) Kim wanted a garage (for all the practical reasons), a basement that she could set up a workshop and stand upright in (again, for all the practical reasons) and storage space for things like golf clubs and her hockey bag. This stone house was darling, but it had none of those things.

It was also a designated heritage property. Our realtor, Jane, who navigated all the fine print for us, seemed confident that it wasn't a deterrent. However, anything we did to the exterior of the house would have to be approved by the Heritage Committee, and these changes would have to be in line with the architectural integrity of the home and history. In fact, this committee would invest 50 percent in any reasonable restoration project, up to five thousand dollars per calendar year.

Neither of us had ever envisioned living in West Galt. To us, the area was a once-in-a-while boozy night at the Nest, a local honky-tonk women's bar housed in an old warehouse on the river (two blocks from the stone cottage), where the DJ still played records in a space no bigger than a phone booth. The two women who owned the Nest turned it into a private club with membership fees (which didn't make it any fancier) and sold hot roast beef sandwiches (leftovers from their Friday slow-cooker dinner) at midnight. There were always urns of coffee and tea (and store-bought cookies) for the designated drivers and lineups for the pool tables. Everyone in the know came to Cambridge to go to the Nest —even from Toronto. Kim and I felt like stragglers, a little late to the party in discovering a different, amiable side of Cambridge. Kim asked if I would be okay living so far away from Toronto. I asked her, "Are you going to be okay without a garage?" We bounced back pros and cons, possibilities for the carriage house, and we both sighed at the thought of lazy afternoons in loungers in the backyard without all the sirens and racket of the city. We put in an offer.

As with all real-estate transactions, we didn't have the leisure of discussing things for very long. The seller's agent called our agent with the news that another offer had come in. It was probably a bluff, but we wanted the house, bluff or not. The tactic worked; we bit and bid and the house was sold—to us.

When we moved in, it was with a crush of company—twenty-six people visited in two days, and all wanted a tour and a beer. In between, we tried to paint every single room at lightning speed. Friends came with other friends, in between the cable guy and the phone guy. It was a house that garnered a lot of interest— everyone wanted to see inside. So, punch-drunk, we toured, painted a bit and toured again. Joleen, a staff member at the McDougall Cottage Historic Site (our stone home's 1858 granite and limestone doppelgänger, half a block away), became an ally. "McDougall Cottage has almost the same footprint," she said, "and I think William Webster, a stonemason, built both."

A clairvoyant friend dropped by. Wendy stopped still when she entered our master bedroom. "I can hear him. On the anvil." She told us: "If you're in the kitchen and feel a shove from behind, don't be alarmed. It's okay—it's a good spirit." And then: "You two will have a big celebration in August." We made note of this.

A neighbour who stopped in with lemon coconut cake asked us to think about joining the Holly Jolly Christmas house tour. "It's so great, you'll love it. Your house is perfect for this. One of the local shops will come in, dress it all up for the holidays, and it's all for charity." When we naively agreed, we were flattered. We had no idea that twelve hundred people were going to be traipsing through our house on the wettest weekend in November. And then there was the hallowed Galt Horticultural Society garden tour. Another neighbour recruited us for that. The garden tour saw another crowd of a hundred people pile into our backyard, tiptoeing around our rare apricot poppies, giant peony bushes, elegant eastern redbuds, parrot tulips, stonecrops, massive bear's breeches and Dr. Seuss–like pompom allium.

When we weren't hosting a hundred picky gardeners in our backyard or twelve hundred people for a weekend, we hung out with fellow Toronto expats Troy and Lori. We had become fast friends over a shared love of old houses and old dogs and beer. They lived in a two-storey stone house almost as old as ours. We agreed, Cambridge *was* a beautiful combo of Carolinian woods, a pleasing downtown, historic buildings and innovation. We swapped trade secrets about stone homes during beer-class intermissions at Grand River Brewing, which was conveniently located halfway between our two houses.

I was having job delusions of grandeur, as per usual (it doesn't take long). I toyed with the idea of working at the brewery, swirling hops and creating fun beer labels. Beer class was so much fun, how could a job there not be? When our house deal was finalized (we bought in November but had a late January close), I made a cold call to the spa manager at Langdon Hall Country House Hotel and Spa, using bragging rights from my employment at the Royal York and the King Edward Hotel, and I scheduled an interview with Julie, even though there was no job available.

It was an eight-kilometre walk, in a slushy combo of freezing rain and fat snowflakes, along the Grand Trunk Trail from our cottage to the plantation-like property of the historic hotel. In the driveway of the hotel, I traded my Converse snow boots for Kim's too-small dress shoes with heels (Kim thought my Converse high-tops were a little too casual for Langdon). Even more graceful, I nearly skidded out flat on the front doorstep as the bellhop ushered me in.

Once inside, I saw that a fire was roaring away in the lobby, snapping, crackling and popping with ambience. A woman in a silk scarf was playing the piano, and two sharp-suited men nursed highball drinks around the snooker table. Uniformed staff walked by in hushed conversation. I loved it all—it was stately, romantic and shooting its five-star rating in every direction. And then along came Miss Wilks and Walter, the hotel's unofficial mascots: two Bernese mountain dogs. I was sold. This was the only place I wanted to work. And I got the job.

But Cambridge provided me with another opportunity to expand my job horizons. What colour *was* my parachute? Keen to marry my interests, I applied to my most realistic whims (in no particular order):

The African Lion Safari. I figured that if I couldn't be in the Congo or Uganda, a Cambridge safari would have to suffice. They had a few zookeeping positions available, and my cover letter was all Congo memories about my time spent as a barista for the chimps at J.A.C.K. I'd be a shoo-in, for sure. But any chance of landing a zookeeper job with only chimp breakfast-making experience was impossible. "We have another job that seems more suited to your skills, though." I pictured myself in the required safari suit and pith helmet and shiny name badge. The interviewer's voice lowered with enticement: "How would you feel about driving a fifty-passenger bus, our zoo train and a boat on our small lake? You could do our public tours!" This woman had just vividly outlined my nightmare. Driving a bus? Full of kids? With zebras and baboons crossing the road all willy-nilly? No thanks.

Dee's Bakery. Dee is rather famous for her butter tarts for this non-secret reason: she bakes the pastry in muffin tins, creating the perfect balance of crust and gooey delight. I wasn't a huge butter tart fan, but I fancied the idea of the sweet heat, the happiness that a bakery brings and experimenting with the fun guts that she put into her tarts (bacon, pretzels, Skor bars). The job wasn't glamorous, but Dee was looking for a part-time tart-shell baker. I could write more travel stuff for Matador and bake tart shells. Win-win. But I didn't even get a call back.

Cambridge Butterfly Conservatory. The posting was for an education programmer, and what a grand place to do that. I had an interview during Bug Week, and after formalities, I was invited to try some fried mealworms, candied ants and chocolate-dipped crickets. Cool! But the position was for the education department that designed curricula for elementary school kids. The interviewer asked, with a giant smile, "So, tell me, what is your favourite age group to work with?" My heart sank. Over ninety, to be honest.

The Grand Café. I pictured myself all sunny behind the counter, serving fair-trade coffee and gluten-free muffins to the architecture school students. But reality check: A 5:30 a.m. start time? I woke up for the chimps at that hour, but nah, not for humans.

City Bakery Café—my last attempt. They were hiring a bagel maker and a pizza baker, morning or afternoon shift. When I dropped off my no-experience resumé, the jaded guy in a tight hairnet behind the counter asked, "What kind of kitchen experience do you have?" I laughed and said, "Nothing formal, but..." and told him some candid story about my Pop-Tart toasting experience. "Don't even bother," he said. "I've already had three hundred people in here, all way more qualified than you."

So, I stuck with the fancy-pants hotel gig at Langdon Hall. Distinct perk: Chef Jason Bangerter and everything he prepared for the staff, like velvety polenta, tender lamb, milkweed salads, precious trout with tiny flower petals and pea shoots.

Once we settled in to our cottage, we took advantage of tiny Galt and everything it offered, from street art festivals to beer-tasting classes at the brewing company to live painting competitions and film nights at the local library. We felt that being part of the Holly Jolly tour and the horticultural society were necessary contributions that we could make as community members and owners of such a storied home.

We supported all the local shop owners. We walked the old electric rail line and every nearby section of the Great Trail. We bought jams and fiery pepperettes at the farmers' market (one of the oldest in Canada), balsamic truffles at the chocolatier, smoked Gouda at the cheese boutique, stiff Americanos at Monigram's, "Elvis" peanut-butter-and-banana cupcakes at the bakery and all sorts of gourmand treats at the upscale grocery store. We picked up spring rolls and Penang curries at our favourite Thai restaurant and drank the lineup of Ontario craft beers at the local pub. We went on owl prowls and ghost walks, and we attended film fests. I found my oyster fix at the buck-a-shuck nights at the historic Cambridge Mill.

Otherwise, Kim and I divided our time between our jobs at the spa and steel mill and being "caretakers of history." Our stone cottage proved to be a crash course in everything for Kim and me. We had an old boiler system to be maintained and repaired, vermiculite in our attic that had to be removed, gardens gone wild to be pruned and intense demolition duties inside and out. The basement was bedrock and full of so many cobwebs that it was like a bat cave. The updates were largely cosmetic, however, and paint was the biggest miracle on the house's tired walls.

In West Galt, undeniably, we had found balance, restorative perennial gardens and a non-intrusive urban lifestyle. There were brilliant orioles and rose-breasted grosbeaks doing flybys in our backyard for the entire month of May. And the church bells. You don't have to have a religious bone to be moved by the sound of these bells on a still, wintry night. But just as we had tamed the gardens into submission and painted every inch into a favourable palette, we sat down at the black walnut-topped kitchen table that Kim had built and sketched out our next plan.

It went like this: Kim would retire, I would quit massage therapy for good, and we would sell this house and move to Prince Edward County. We had been biding time in Cambridge. Our friends and family knew this but still couldn't believe we were ready to give it all up so quickly. I'd found my perfect nomad lover, and we were ready to start looking for our next watering hole.

17.

We Sold Our House on Facebook

KIM DID RETIRE, I quit massage therapy for good, and we sold our house on Facebook. But as much as we wanted to have a forwarding address in Prince Edward County ("the County"), the real-estate market said otherwise.

We wanted to sell first, mostly because of the horror stories out there about carrying two properties. It's a goofy guessing game about what's best—to sell or buy first. Both can leave you in a pickle in a hurry. Kim wanted to sell first, mostly due to her Capricorn stronghold about financial security and rational decision-making. Being a Virgo, I leaned heavily on my golden trait of nothing being left to chance. I wanted to buy a red-brick church in the County six months before we sold our cottage, before Kim had even retired, because I believed this church was *the one*! It wasn't going to sit on the market or return to it any time soon. But when we went to see it, the dream evaporated. It was right on the highway, and the traffic was heavy and noisy. Inside, we both felt like we had entered a circus funhouse with slanting floors.

The market was so hot that putting in a clause like "purchase conditional on sale of current home" would not fly. One agent said County homes were being purchased over the phone by Toronto investors who waived everything—financing, home inspection—and they were buying without conditions. I hated to think that we would miss out on our dream house because we were waiting to sell ours first. Because our sale would be private, the saving grace was that maybe we could negotiate a closing date that would work in our favour. If we found a house sooner, maybe the buyers would accept a shorter close.

What we knew for certain was that we didn't want to use a real-estate agent this time. We wanted to do something unconventional. Kim and I toyed with the idea of raffling our house off, much like the plot of the 1996 movie *Spitfire Grill*. I'd spent most of my life selling strange things and was a serial fundraiser. Wouldn't you buy a $155 ticket with the possibility of winning a house that only required you to arrange your furniture and fill your champagne glasses? I loved the romantic notion of it all. I investigated the idea deeper and was reassured about the popularity and success of such ventures. But could we pull it off in tiny Galt, Ontario?

Kim and I both watched enough HGTV to know the math, logistics and obstacles of selling a home. With our PhD in *Property Brothers, House Hunters International, Fixer Upper* and *Million Dollar Listing New York*, we were confident. Combined, Kim and I had already spent 14,786 hours on realtor.ca, before our house had even sold. We wanted to be part of bucking the standard. Why just have a garage sale anymore? You can sell your whole house! Kim and I opted to craft a post for Facebook. "House for Sale: Ours!"

All we had to do was hand the official paperwork over to a lawyer and the deal would be done for just under a thousand bucks.

The condensed version is—after a big splash on Facebook and over nine hundred visitors to the blog post, we did it. Thanks to the powers of social media and a friend of a friend of a friend, we found our buyer. There was no messy bidding war, no hair pulling, no raffle legalities to contend with. Our buyers simply liked our Facebook post and sent a private message to coordinate a viewing. When they arrived, we shared some small talk and encouraged them to enjoy the bottle of wine we left on the kitchen table and truly experience the house. We wanted the couple to have the freedom to feel and engage with our home in a way you can't with a time-keeping realtor or homeowners on your heels. All we asked was that they sent us a text when they were leaving. Kim and I bided time at the pub across the river. Two hours passed. When they texted us, the bottle of wine was empty and they were in love—with each other, the wine and our house. As we signed papers over cocktails at Langdon Hall Country House Hotel and Spa a few days later, the couple remarked, "This is so civilized." And *they* said it couldn't be done.

The couple who bought our house in May were happy with an August 1 close, and we figured three months was ample time to find a new home. Kim and I had unknowingly just entered the buyer's market at the worst possible time. Prince Edward County was experiencing "mad wine disease," as everyone from Toronto (and their bearded hipster brother) wanted a hunk of real estate there in the County; it was the Niagara wine region's trendier cousin.

At least we weren't buying in Toronto. The average home price in 2017 in the Greater Toronto Area hit $916,567—up 33.2 percent from 2016. While Toronto homeowners cashed out of the city, they were now heading up to our desired territory with even fatter wallets. Waterfront properties in nearby Muskoka, Haliburton and Orillia saw a property value surge of 51.4 percent over a year. I'm not fabulous at math, but I knew we were being outbid before we even began. Real-estate agents reported what we already knew: "Everybody's looking for a four-hundred-foot frontage lot or a tear-down." Contractors were already booked for two years in advance. Even if we did find something, it would have to be immediately livable, because no one would be available to flip a three-season to a year-round home for us.

In cottage country, entry-level homes in Bracebridge and Gravenhurst in the desirable $229,000 to $279,000 bracket were selling for $30,000 to $40,000 over asking price. The president of Royal LePage Lakes of Muskoka said there were cottages netting thirty showings in a day. Lucky ducks who sold their former crack houses in Toronto for a million in almost-gentrified areas like the Junction or Queen East were buying fifty-acre farms in Haliburton and wineries in the County without having to apply for a mortgage, and they still had money in the bank.

We worried that maybe we had over-romanticized the County, but still we persevered (wishing we had bought a crack house way back when). I had launched into "we're locals" mode quite swiftly, dog-earing pages of the local papers and brochures as Kim drove. I told her where we could go see alpacas get sheared. September was the big cheese festival in nearby Picton. In the fall we could go to the bird observatory and help band migrating saw-whet owls. We were hooked. The County was vibrating with possibility. It had everything from wineries to sausage makers to beekeepers to lavender fields. There were old-timey post offices, tiny library branches, bike trails and independent bookstores. Kim pictured us stand-up paddle boarding and walking the Millennium Trail end to end with some refuelling stops at wineries.

Everyone we met was chasing a dream or already sinking their teeth into it. There were countless galleries, colourful cafés, bike shops and over forty wineries (this has since doubled). There are bed-and-breakfast owners building octagon-shaped homes with straw-bale insulation. North America's first off-grid vineyard was here, saddled up alongside North America's first vegan-certified winery. Stuff was going on! People networked as a hobby and knew each other by their dog or their beat-up pickup. The passion was tangible— this was a community populated with a surplus of talent, knowledge, nerdy obsessions and ambition. We wanted to live there.

As minted caretakers of history, Kim and I appreciated how old barns were repurposed into wineries and gallery spaces. We'd be mentally well nourished and stimulated in the County. We had the vision, right down to the garlic-braiding workshops and glass-blowing classes on Sunday afternoons. We were ready to take pastoral to the next level.

All we wanted was this: front-row sunsets, a body of water (pond, lake, creek) and a walking-distance winery with a wood-fired pizza oven. Also: polished cement floors with radiant heating, a Japanese soaker tub, some Carrara marble, a fieldstone fireplace,

Raffles, Auctions, Contests and More
The Humble Heart Goat Dairy and Creamery in Elkmont, Alabama, opted to raffle off their establishment. The Rock Spring Farm in Essex County, Virginia, was raffling off their thirty-eight-acre horse farm. There was even a movie theatre on the raffle block. At the time I was researching the process and the fine print of raffles, I found a link to a seaside cinema (Cape Ann Cinema and Stage in Gloucester, Massachusetts) that could be won in a 250-word essay contest. There was a B & B in Maine being "sold" by the owner, who'd won it in an essay contest back in 1993 and wanted to share the karma all over again.

A Whitby, Ontario, couple who owned a waterfront property in Kingston—a gated house with turrets, an elevator, a cedar grove and two thousand feet of waterfront—opted to cash out with an auction. The minimum bid was three hundred thousand dollars. There were thirteen offers, and it sold for double that. •

a loft bedroom, a bookshelf with one of those sliding ladders, a Wolf stove, a workshop taller than Smurf height for Kim and floor-to-ceiling windows that retract and open up to a cedar deck overlooking the above-mentioned millpond, lake, burbling creek. That's all.

We didn't think we were being too picky about things. After living in so many apartments, houses and jungle huts in our combined lives, we knew all the things we didn't want: wind turbines, train tracks, highways, carpenter ants, trailer park views, erosion, black walnut trees, access roads designed for snowmobiles and ATVs versus cars and/or property taxes over five thousand dollars.

Our greatest difficulty, in fact, was our freedom. Because we had no geographical boundaries (due to work), we were truly free-range chickens. We had no family ties holding us down, with all of our immediate family members living all over the map, from Banff to Charlottetown. Our friends were peppered in all the places in between, so there wasn't a single depository that could anchor us. There was nowhere else we wanted to live but the fabled County.

Our closing date was approaching at warp speed, so we began to recalibrate and refine our wish list. First, we were willing to forgo water. Then sunsets. Eventually, the wish list read simply: Something in Prince Edward County. We went from looking at shipping-container homes from a Montreal company to tiny-house living to three-thousand-square-foot manors "perfect for a B & B start-up." By mid-June the panic set in. "We're going to have to put stuff into storage," Kim said. She was right, but I felt that we were giving up by deciding to do it. We booked a container to arrive the second week in July. We'd have a week to fill it and then it would be sent to our new address—whenever that happened. If it was going to the County, it would ring in at nine hundred dollars. Anywhere beyond that and the tickertape kept going up. We had no choice.

So much for "freedom." Freedom was feeling suffocated when we were boxing everything up with nowhere to go. We started looking at vacant lots and met with builders, pricing out an open-concept fifteen-hundred-square-foot design. We took pictures of a board-and-batten three-car garage near Black River with a cute cupola that was exactly what we wanted for a house. The numbers rolled in around three hundred thousand dollars, plus land, plus septic, plus digging for a well, hydro hookup, driveway, tree clearing, et cetera. I trembled a little with all the et ceteras that couldn't be fully accounted for until the process was underway.

Kim continued to sketch out floor plans, and we looked at prefab designs. If we built, we would get exactly what we wanted. Friends began to ask, "Why do you guys want to buy a house at all? Why don't you just sell everything off and travel? You love travelling." Yes, we loved to travel, but we also wanted a home base where we could hang the gallery of travel pictures that we'd collected over the years. We had cool door knockers and no doors. Kim had a workshop full of tools, and I had a bookshelf of beloved books, a cowhide and a vintage typewriter. We had a wood signpost with the names of all the places we've been to hammered onto it, from Iceland to Zanzibar. We wanted a home, a personal museum of "us." We wanted our own stellar view, a wood-burning fireplace, an island, a royal bed with a five-star thread count and eggs Benny in the morning.

We'd settled on "soft country." (This is how I had sold Kim on Zanzibar: "It's like soft Africa. No malaria, no lions—actually, there's nothing that can eat you there.") In our soft country, we'd still have

A wrong turn on a gravel road introduced us to the Barn Quilt Project. There are more than sixty "barn quilts" across the County, most measuring eight square feet, hung on local barns. Based on traditional quilting patterns, the designs of a single quilt block are painted on plywood and are a tribute to Ontario's disappearing landscapes: old timber-frame barns and farms. •

"city-type" services like recycling and compost pickup, mailbox delivery and a firepit we could use without suburban watchdogs calling in a complaint about a backyard campfire without a permit. I wanted to be remote, but not off a flight path (and definitely close to a large airport so we could conveniently jet off on a whim if there was a handsome seat sale). We both wanted to be walking distance to some things (a library, a cup of sugar, some whisky) and less than ten kilometres to a grocery store. And we wanted privacy after so much suburbia. More bird and butterfly traffic than cars.

Luckily, Kim and I had both wrapped up at work in July. It made house hunting a whole lot easier than joining the weekend traffic heading north. Countless times, a listing would be on the market on Monday and gone by the time we could get back up to the County. We drove three hours one way and sometimes returned three hours back, trying to save on our growing last-minute hotel costs.

We looked at more old churches, old schoolhouses, Pan-Abodes, stone farmhouses, Confederation log homes, DIY disasters, gated communities, passive solar homes, kit homes and a house with a creepy doll collection. We looked at Devil Lake (overpriced, dated), a Viceroy in Shallow Lake (carpenter ants and bathtub in bedroom), a Prinyer's Cove lot (view of cement factory), Tett Crescent (soupy lot) and a Napanee cottage that smelled like we had just stepped into a smoker's lung. And then our search grew wider, encompassing tiny towns with Icelandic settler cemeteries and fall fairs with a "Most Personable Hamster" category. I had to Wiki some of the little towns to see where they were. We extended our search to Pelee Island, Wolfe Island, Amherst Island...

After we sold our house, we looked at eighty-seven houses and lots and spent a year living in our friends' barn.

18.

A Year on Caberneigh Farm

WE WERE DRINKING a growler of amber beer with our friends PJ and Nicole, watching their free-range chickens decimate a stale coffee cake and some strawberry bums. "You guys know you're welcome to stay here on the farm if you can't find a place before your close," Nicole said. Kim and I were so certain that we'd find a place that we hardly entertained the offer. But when the shipping container with all our worldly stuff left our driveway in Galt and we had a week until closing, we decided that the farm was a solid option. We took advantage of their offer before anyone (especially them) changed their mind. "It's just for a few weeks," we kept reassuring ourselves. I kept my clothes in bags, mostly out of superstition. I wanted to be ready to go once our house revealed itself.

Kim and I had been on the farm for two weeks when I was offered a job for which I hadn't even applied. The publisher of *Harrowsmith* magazine, Yolanda Thornton, had sent an email asking if we could talk. After another day of exploring lousy listings, I checked my emails and didn't think too deeply about the request from *Harrowsmith*. I had submitted a story about Fronterra, the farm-camp brewery in Prince Edward County, which was to be published in their fall issue. When I called Yolanda the next morning, I figured she was calling to get my new address. Instead, she chatted at length about the magazine's brand, about its mantra (simplicity, sustainability) and how the editor-in-chief thought I was a great brand ambassador. She talked about how the publishing house started, her past involvement with *Harrowsmith* and the new direction she was steering the brand toward. *Wow,* I thought, *this conversation is really involved for just an address update.* "So, Jules," she said, "would you be interested in the role of editor-in-chief at *Harrowsmith*?"

I was stunned. "I thought you were calling for an address change to send me a copy of the fall edition," I blurted. I explained that Kim and I were looking for a house, so I had no idea where we were going to end up. Would I be required to physically be somewhere? "The beauty of this position is that it's remote. Wherever you end up, you can do the job from home."

Home. We needed a home!

Editor-in-chief, though? What did that even mean? I wasn't familiar with any of the software programs she rhymed off. I frantically copied down all the skills I lacked: InDesign, CP style, proficiency on a Mac platform, Google Analytics, three to five years in a magazine or newspaper environment, monthly metric reports, managing a digital CMS (I still don't know what this is). I had all the soft skills down pat (strong digital and social media storytelling ability, familiarity with key topics in the magazine's scope and cultural landscape, strong written communication and the ability to work autonomously). I told Yolanda I needed to digest it all and would call her after the weekend.

Kim returned to the barn just as I ended the call. "What did she want? Are you going to write something else for them?"

I was still shell-shocked—I don't even know what kind of expression I had slapped on my face when I said, "She asked if I wanted to be the editor-in-chief."

Kim was immediately enthusiastic. No one seemed too bothered about my lack of editorial skills. I explained that it was a remote position (the maker or breaker for me) and I could work anywhere. "Do it!" Kim cheered me on, as she always has with my writing adventures. "There's nothing to lose. She's right—you can learn a lot of that stuff on the job. Let's celebrate!"

Kim grabbed two beers, and my one-month retirement period ended just like that. I became editor-in-chief of *Harrowsmith* and navigated new software and networked with freelancers in between scrolling through new house listings. Kim took on dozens of unexpected roles at the farm, learning the fine art of giving a pot-bellied pig a pedicure, driving a John Deere tractor and winterizing two Airstreams. She didn't expect to fell trees, jar honey or become part of an adult 4-H experience. Soon she was building bat houses and birdhouses and even a mid-century-modern bird feeder. We didn't expect to be bottle-feeding tiny mewing rescue kittens or wrangling chickens at dusk.

During our year on Caberneigh Farm, we learned some farming lessons:

1. The dogs and pig will never admit to having already been fed.

2. Farm dogs like Halls lemon lozenges—an entire Costco-size bag in one go. No cough necessary. They also like to eat marshmallows, even if they are still in the plastic bag. (*Insert Elvis the ol' hound dog here as prime suspect.)

3. Horses sometimes like to let themselves out for a walk at three in the morning.

4. Sneezing can be considered a sport when living in a barn.

5. If you're too lazy to go into town for butter, mayonnaise subs in quite nicely, smeared on the exterior slices of a grilled cheese sandwich.

6. Pigs like Scotch mints. Or at least Olive does.

7. Chickens will eat chicken—an entire beer-can chicken carcass, even. And mice. In one gulp.

8. Chickens will wrangle themselves. Wait until dusk, and they'll all make their way home and into the coop without being asked.

9. Harvesting honey on-site means happy hour can take on a whole new flavour. (Try a Bee Sting: 2 ounces of dark rum, 1 tablespoon of honey, juice of half a lemon. Shake and serve on ice.)

10. If you have a bee sting (not the cocktail), meat tenderizer will take the sting out of the bite. •

PJ and Nicole hadn't expected us to be camped out there for an entire year, either.

We soon earned an endearing nickname: the Barn Cats. Our new headquarters were dubbed the "barn-dominium." There were marvellous perks to living on a farm. Eggnog season had never been so satisfying! Eggs became a serious staple, especially because our "kitchen" was a skillet and a BBQ. The panini maker had a good workout over the year as Kim and I learned the fine art of making everything into a fabulous pressed sandwich. It was like fancy camping, though we missed having a stove and oven and fanta-sized aloud about when we'd finally be in our new home, sim-mering French onion soup, boiling corn on the cob and prepping butter-chicken pizzas.

When we weren't fantasizing about a stove or preheating an oven or having a pullout freezer, we were dreaming about our bed. Driving up to Perth on another real-estate run, Kim and I decided to count how many different beds we had slept in since we sold our house in August 2016 (forty-three). During our house-hunting mission, we slept on innumerable inflatable (or no longer inflatable) mattresses, in tents, in Airstreams and at both Super 8s and five-star hotels. We slept in so many guest bedrooms that we became mattress experts.

Still, we kept looking for our home. Our only real-estate intermissions were when we went to China, Thailand and St. Lucia. Each time we went away, we thought, this is when it's going to happen. We're going to come home from Bangkok and our house will appear. We heard all the stories about how easily all of our friends and their friends and their friends' friends found their houses. PJ and Nicole looked at one property—Caberneigh Farm. Kim's sister looked at one house. What was our big problem? What was taking us so long? Most normal people are forced to look in a very tight radius for a house. They want a good school district for their kids. They want a nearby dog park and a grocery store. Maybe a gym. The house has to be right for a growing family or needs to have an in-law suite.

While we learned many life lessons on the farm, we also learned what not to say to someone looking for a house:

Have you thought of building?

It will be worth the wait.

You'll know it when you find it.

Take your time; you've waited this long.

Do you have a real-estate agent?

You're so lucky. No bills to pay. No mortgage. No grass to cut. Lucky!

We felt far from lucky. The fall market sucked. Thanksgiving passed and cottages were closed up and not listed as promised. The new year was as frozen as the Frontenac. The market had turned on its head, and now homeowners were afraid to sell, because there was nothing on the market for them to buy.

We were no longer going to do this without real-estate agents. In fact, we had a real-estate agent in every port: Jane in Fergus,

Barb in Perth, Heath in the Frontenac, Carey and Gail in the County, Ashley in Tobermory, Meirion in Warkworth, Diane in Bayfield and Chris in Westport. We had Jamie and Cathy, a realtor and a builder, a husband-and-wife combo team. We had Chris who sold container homes, an agent on Meyers Island, and the guys from Armitage eager to design a passive solar build for us. But no house. Our route on the map was a Spirograph, as we clocked forty thousand kilometres in no time. Everywhere we wanted to be was three hours from the farm, and we kept stretching ourselves further.

We had lots of ideas about where and what we could do. Were we supposed to move to Quebec's Magdalen Islands? We loved the Maggies and the colourful homes dotted along Havre-Aubert. There was a purple one I had my eye on. We could go there—make an offer and live happily ever after learning how to make cheese curds and smoke herring. I'd become a Farley Mowat expert and run literary tours up to Old Harry, where Mowat liked to hang out. Kim could make things out of razor clams, and we could build a doghouse out of sand dollars.

We could be lighthouse keepers like Caroline Woodward. I'd recently read her memoir, *Light Years*. What if we auctioned off everything in our shipping container and walked the Camino de Santiago? My former boss and her husband had quit their jobs, sold their house in Toronto and bought a property in Mérida, Mexico. I thought of everyone in our circle and what "home" had come to mean for them. Michelle had spent years in frozen Nunavut; Chantal in Mauritania, in northwest Africa. I thought of Merryde with her homes in both Africa and Australia. I couldn't help but think of Antoine in Melbourne, Australia. Part of me wanted to drift off to Africa again. We could buy a little coffee plantation and tell tall tales over gin-and-tonic sundowners, with a Rhodesian ridgeback or two at our feet. We could wear khakis and eat antelope and write long letters by candlelight.

We wanted something so basic. A house. People buy them all the time. In the past I was content to be a drifter. Kim and I wanted to travel *and* have a home base. We wanted to drop anchor but still be able to take off to Papua New Guinea, Saint-Pierre and Miquelon, or the hot-air balloon fest in Albuquerque.

By the end of March, we'd been on the farm for eight months. Almost a pregnancy. I self-diagnosed: I definitely had *zugunruhe,* a German word for "migration restlessness," the stirring before moving. Our crush on Prince Edward County was finally over. We turned our search to the north on a whim, and then we could taste it: the cedar, the stardust, the loon feathers and birch and limestone. Was it really too remote? From who or what?

"We've looked everywhere. We have gone from a budget of $250,000 to $450,000 and there's still nothing." We were defeated.

"The only other possible place is that one halfway up to Tobermory."

"The over-budget one?"

"Yeah. The open-concept one on the lake. Something has to give already."

Kim zoomed in on Bruce Peninsula. "This is the one I meant."

We crawled through the pictures, scrutinizing and analyzing every angle. It looked promising, but so had the eighty-seven houses we'd already looked at.

I phoned our agent and told her that the Bruce Peninsula was back on our horizon. The home had been on the market for days, and the northern market was starting to thaw. "You should come and see it very soon," she advised. Kim and I went the very next day. The skies were slate grey and miserable. But the house? It had a glow of its own. We pulled up the long driveway that split the cedars and towering pines as a pileated woodpecker swooped in and out of the verdant blur. Chickadees chattered away and bounced in for a closer look.

Was this our home?

19.

You Are Here

IT WAS *EVERYTHING*. Right down to the cupola and weather vane.

We wanted privacy but not no man's land. We wanted sunsets and a lake. Vaulted ceilings, an open floor plan, a soaker tub, hardwood floors, a workshop, a garage. And it was all in a designated Dark Sky Community. We'd be living in a UNESCO World Heritage Site. There was a cedar boardwalk along the still lake, six miles of trails and an old logging road through the mossy hinterland. There was even a Little Library (one I could stock with back issues of *Harrowsmith*) just fifty feet from our driveway. With transom windows, a walk-through pantry, a pocket-door powder room and a gas fireplace, it was all check, check, check. The board-and-batten exterior was in our colour palette (dove grey), and the back deck had suntanning, recreational reading and gin and tonics written all over it. We would be seven kilometres from the town of Lion's Head, which had a marina, farmers' market, Home Hardware, Foodland, LCBO, vintage café, access to the Bruce Trail, and the historic Lion's Head Inn pub.

We did the expected real-estate dance of give and take, and within days, Ashley called to say the house was ours. We had a 2,750-square-foot house with four bathrooms. It was bigger than we ever imagined or wanted, but it had everything we needed: a tiny dock with front-row seats to wide-screen sunsets. No grass to cut. No Master Gardener gardens to break our backs. There was no exhaustive list of changes or major structural things to deal with. The house was bright and freeing, the kind of place you walk into and take a deep breath.

Buying a house is a crazy, compressed thing. It's identical to a first date. You have a coffee, try to act casual, try to contain your excitement—but you're still cautious and looking for potential red flags. You have a good hour with the house, getting to know a little about its age, history, style, perks and downfalls. At the end of that hour, after you look at a house that's for sale, you have to make a major life-altering, bank-account-dwindling decision. After one precious hour of flitting about the surface, you have to say, "I do!" Or not. And your second date is with a lawyer and/or house inspector and a real-estate agent. It's like getting married on your second date.

Eighty-eight houses later, we had found our wow. As our psychic friend had predicted, we *would* have a big celebration in August. We moved out of our stone cottage in August of 2016, and we moved in to our Lion's Head house on August 1, 2017.

By nightfall on the first of August, Kim and I had already painted the master bedroom and office a cracked peppercorn colour. We drank Hinterland bubbly from the County on the dock at sunset, in a pinch-me state. At midnight, we had our first dinner in our house: beer and chocolate chip cookies. When we finally stopped and flopped back on our inflatable mattress, everything was vibrating. I could hear the blood circulating in my head and eyeballs.

Our shipping container arrived August 2. The next day, we rented a U-Haul and retrieved the rest of our worldly stuff in a marathon six-hundred-kilometre round trip. We gathered stuff from all our outposts. We had dress clothes and winter jackets, duvets and linens, my precious manuscripts, published work, tax stuff, antique snowshoes, industrial bar stools, a doormat ("Let's Stay Home"), hiking poles, barnboard, gourd birdhouse, laser level, angle grinder, two carry-on suitcases and a box of booze (wine from Prince Edward County) at my parents' house. At Kim's sister's house, we picked up all our stereo stuff, our flat-screen TV, a Gluckenstein patio set we had bought at a close-out sale in June, post spikes, more Ikea frames, a delicate horse print, Adirondack chairs, a timber fireplace mantel, more barnboard and square steel tube legs.

On the third day, we heard a screech owl, spotted a coiled mas-sasauga rattler on the logging trail and watched the antics of a red-breasted nuthatch bopping about while we nursed coffee on the front step. A bald eagle cruised overhead on a thermal. A beaver paddled by at dusk. We witnessed a red squirrel carry her four young from a birdhouse to the great outdoors, all legs and tail. Four garter snakes sunbathed on our front deck—we named them Purse, Clutch, Belt and Boots.

We resurrected our stuff in a week-long stretch that felt like Christmas morning on repeat.

So, is home a person, a place or a thing?

For me, finding home has been a map-less journey that's gone sideways, backwards and dreamily forwards, just like a Spirograph doodle. There are roots that run deep, exes and *Oh!*s, U-Hauls and an entire alphabet of postal codes in between. Had I gone to Melbourne with Antoine to bake bread and not moved to Vancouver with a thousand dollars in my bank account to live with the cat in the shoebox, I wouldn't have gone to the jungle to live in a house with no walls, and I wouldn't have ended up in Dunnville. I wouldn't have met Kim on the boat in Lake Ontario or met her again seven years later. I wouldn't have moved to Toronto and then out to Abbotsford, BC, if I hadn't become a massage therapist, which happened in Dunnville. And if I hadn't moved out to BC to be with Cagney, I wouldn't have found myself doodling colouring books in Uganda or making breakfast for chimps in the Congo. I definitely wouldn't have landed back in Toronto and gone to Amsterdam with Kim. If I had gone to Maui instead and lived in a yurt with the monkeys, I wouldn't have bought an old stone house in Galt and lived on a farm for nearly a year. Or moved here, to Lion's Head.

While the technical explanation of a Spirograph is rather complicated and as dry as a sun-dried tomato, the mathematical roulette curves were originally intended to prevent bank forgeries. This wasn't something I knew until now—to me a Spirograph was the start of a pencil point with no end. Everything was connected so long as you kept your sweaty hand steady.

The Spirograph design is based on epitrochoids and hypotrochoids that roll around a fixed circle. There are interior circles and exterior ones, and a circle of radius. This has been my life, for sure.

Everyone assumes house eighty-eight will be our forever home—how can it not be? We nailed everything on our checklist. Would we be willing to ride on the real-estate roller coaster again? Probably. Kim and I both get twitchy in one place after a certain amount of time. The desire to flip spaces into "us" is a weird gravitational pull that luckily we both share.

The Spirograph pattern would predict another move, and the circle of radius that Kim and I inhabit is expanding. In September

2019 we are modern-day eloping. Meaning, we have let everyone in our inner circle know that we're getting married, but they're not invited. We plan to kiss the cod and each other in Heart's Content, Newfoundland.

I know this much is true: Kim is my anchor, and this house is home for now.

We are free to a good home, with room for improvement, together.

Suggested Reading

In random order, just as these books fell into my lap, I'd recommend integrating these titles into your *curricula vitae*.

Choose Your Own Adventure, a series by R.A. Montgomery and Edward Packard. There are 184 titles, and the collection is a reminder that every single day you can choose your very own adventure and start anew.

Another Lost Whole Moose Catalogue (Harbour Publishing). It's out of stock and out of print (1991), but there's an original and third edition to track down too—the *Great Northern Lost Moose Catalogue* (1997). "It's the classic '70s statement about preserving a unique northern bush lifestyle." And you *can* just read the statements wherever you are, not necessarily in the northern bush, as I previously believed.

A House Somewhere: Tales of Life Abroad, edited by Don George and Anthony Sattin. If you've ever fancied yourself under the Tuscan sun like Diane Lane, here's even more inspiration to sell it all.

Belonging by Isabel Huggan. During my existential Toronto years, I bought six copies of this book for everyone on my parallel.

Open House by Elizabeth Berg. When "home" becomes a collapsed house of cards.

The Glass Castle by Jeannette Walls. It's the best memoir ever written. Anyone who disputes this probably hates kittens too.

The House of All Sorts by Emily Carr. Carr was a remarkable woman with a love of dogs and tall trees, who struggled a lifetime in pursuit of her talent.

A Fool and Forty Acres by Geoff Heinricks. This one was a prerequisite to living in Prince Edward County. It made me want to grow grapes as much as *Out of Africa* inspired me to own a coffee plantation.

Out of Africa by Isak Dinesen (Karen Blixen). This was part of my I'm-only-reading-about-Africa-before-I-go-to-Uganda phase. It will make you long for Africa, even if you've never been.

The Poisonwood Bible by Barbara Kingsolver. I roared through this one between Amsterdam and touchdown in Entebbe. It's about an American missionary family trying to claim Congolese jungle real estate as their "home" (and God's property too).

A House in the Sky by Amanda Lindhout and Sarah Corbett. Lindhout's memoir details how she endured a harrowing fifteen months of being held captive by Islamic insurgents in Somalia, and how she nearly forgot the security and safety of "home." It's haunting and will change you.

Falling Backwards by Jann Arden. Jann calls Canada home, and she is as Canadian as maple syrup, a Cowichan sweater and a prairie dog. This memoir will rip your heart open and then stitch it up with hope.

Light Years: Memoir of a Modern Lighthouse Keeper by Caroline Woodward. Your romantic notions about lighthouse keeping might be tarnished, but this is a gorgeous account of life at sea, in a lighthouse.

They Left Us Everything: A Memoir by Plum Johnson. If you ever wondered about what happens to all those knick-knacks and paddywhacks when the matriarch dies, you'll enjoy Plum Johnson's raw read on sifting through an emotional attic.

The Five Love Languages by Gary Chapman. If you want to be on the same page and sleep in the same bed, learn your lingua franca and find a native speaker of your love language. Otherwise, your relationship will sound a whole lot like Charlie Brown's teacher.

Soundtrack (in somewhat chronological order)

"She's Like the Wind"—Patrick Swayze

"Mimi on the Beach"—Jane Siberry

"Closer to Fine"—Indigo Girls

"Take My Breath Away"—Berlin

"Everywhere"—Fleetwood Mac

"Go West"—Pet Shop Boys

"True Colours"—Cyndi Lauper

"Beauty"—Shaye

"The First Cut Is the Deepest"—Sheryl Crow

Afterglow—Sarah McLachlan (entire album)

"I Will Love Again"—Lara Fabian

"Africa"—Toto

"I've Been Doing OK"—Tucker Finn

"The Gambler"—Kenny Rogers

"Could I Be Your Girl?"—Jann Arden

"Thing for You"—Jann Arden

"All the Days"—Jann Arden (do you see the pattern yet?)

"Psycho Killer"—Talking Heads

"(You Want to) Make a Memory"—Bon Jovi

(REPEAT)

Acknowledgements/ Shout-outs

REESE WITHERSPOON SAID something great about "mothering" when she was interviewed about her new lifestyle slash cookbook. *Whiskey in a Teacup* serves as a tribute not only to her grandmother, but to all the southern women who have influenced her in some way. We grow taller and braver because of the love of our mothers, and there are always other pivotal women too—whether you call it mothering or mentoring (or sometimes a crush), they are part of our matrix.

Though you might not find all of their names in this book, they were there (and they are here!), cheerleading me the loudest. I have to thank dozens. (Yes, this is my Golden Globes speech and the orchestra will no doubt cut in.)

Thank you (and a ten-minute fireworks display) to Vici Johnstone and Holly Vestad at Caitlin Press for believing that my memoir deserved a bigger audience. Applause for my editor, Susan Safyan, who massaged the kinks out of the manuscript and streamlined my ultra-marathon-worthy run-on sentences. A generous pour of champagne for my copy editor, Christine Savage, who sniffed out all my grammatical faux pas and happily jumped into my time machine of Jordache jeans, waterbeds and Tahiti Treat.

To Suzanne Chapin, who drove me home with a dead bat that I wanted to pickle in formaldehyde when I was eight, and who called me every Sunday in my teen years. Thanks to my grade twelve English teacher, Joan Hamlin, for suggesting that my writing was like a whitewater rafting adventure—perhaps I could restrain myself to a paddle on a calm lake? To Sharon Gilmour for embedding an idea that became my career trajectory when she said, "Massage is the greatest gift you can give someone." To Rene Franklin, for letting me into your home (and cottage) when I had no postal code. To Rebecca Wigod, for handing me my first book review job, at the *Vancouver Sun*.

To Rona Maynard, the former editor of *Chatelaine*, for inviting *me* to be her guest blogger. I just about fainted from panic over using the wrong tense, but thank you for your confidence in my writing and for insisting that I seek refinement over raw. To Heidi Dreimuller, Farrah Easton, Sara DeRuiter and Julie Simcox for offering me gainful employment during my trips to the Congo, Colombia, Uganda, Zanzibar, et cetera (fill in the blank here: _____).

To Jann Arden, for telling me years ago that I need to jump out of my skin.

To everyone who bought a crappy tie-dye T-shirt, painted flowerpot or beeswax candle, or whatever I was selling at the time to finance my next great adventure—thank you.

To my family, the Original Five, who have learned to say, "I don't want to read about this on Facebook—or in a book!"

And, to Kim, always. My soon-to-be wife.

JULES TORTI writes about the best things in life: birds, beer, beaches, burgers and books (in no particular order). Her work has been published in *Cottage Life*, *Now*, *Fashion*, the *Vancouver Sun*, the *Globe and Mail*, Mabuhay, *Coast Mountain Culture Magazine*, Matador Network, *Massage Therapy Canada* and *Canadian Running*. She contributes regularly to Realtor.ca's blog *Living Room* and is currently the editor in chief of *Harrowsmith* magazine. In other lives she has made breakfast for chimpanzees, illustrated colouring books for the Jane Goodall Institute, won a flight to Costa Rica in an essay contest and had short stories published in a dozen lesbian anthologies. Her first handsome paycheque was for a lesbian erotica story published in *The Mammoth Book of Erotica* (Running Press, 2000). She now lives happily ever after with her partner on the 45th parallel north, exactly half way between the equator and the North Pole, in Lion's Head, Ontario.

Other Books by Dagger Editions

✢

Food Was Her Country by Marusya Bociurkiw
978-1-987915-64-8 | Memoir
Lambda Literary Finalist—Lesbian Memoir/Biography

How can a god-fearing Catholic, immigrant mother
and her godless, bohemian daughter possibly find common ground?
Food Was Her Country is the story of a mother, her queer daughter
and their tempestuous culinary relationship.

————

What the Mouth Wants by Monica Meneghetti
978-1-987915-35-8 | Memoir
Lambda Literary Finalist—Bisexual Non-fiction
Bisexual Book Awards Winner (tie)—Memoir

This mouth-watering, intimate and sensual memoir traces
Meneghetti's unique life journey as she ultimately redefines and recreates
family and identity according to her own alternative vision.

————

Flight Instructions for the Commitment Impaired by Nicola Harwood
978-1-987915-14-3 | Memoir

Outrageous, sad and very funny, Harwood's memoir describes
how she and her girlfriend, a sex-positive butch/femme couple, attempt
to build a relationship with their foster child, Antwan, an eleven-year-
old African American boy with gender identity issues.

————

Swelling with Pride: Queer Conception and Adoption Stories
edited by Sara Graefe
978-1-987915-84-6 | Non-fiction Anthology

An anthology with more than twenty-five creative non-fiction
LGBTQ2 authors from across North America, *Swelling with Pride*
celebrates queer families and the myriad of ways queer folk
embark upon their parenting journeys.

Oscar of Between: A Memoir of Identity and Ideas by Betsy Warland
978-1-987915-16-7 | Memoir

A contemporary *Orlando*, *Oscar of Between* extends beyond
Warland's personal narrative, pushing the boundaries of form and genre.
By doing so, Warland invents new ways of seeing ourselves.

————

Acquired Community by Jane Byers
978-1-987915-22-8 | Poetry
2017 Goldie Winner for Poetry

Acquired Community is both a collection of narrative poems
about seminal moments in North American queer history and a series
of first-person poems that act as a touchstone to compare the
narrator's coming out experience within the larger context of the
gay liberation movement.

————

Playing Into Silence by Tina Biello
978-1-987915-78-5 | Poetry

Biello unearths just about everything from beneath the
Alberta ground: dinosaur bones, a family's firstborn, missing cows.
A voice from within the Prairies, *Playing Into Silence* is a
look back at a dry time in lesbian identity.

————

All Violet by Rani Rivera
978-1-987915-55-6 | Poetry

In *All Violet*, a young woman chronicles the experience of
living on the margins, in spaces where body and mind are flayed
by guilt, disappointments, and betrayals.